Easy Orchids

**Simple Secrets
for Glorious Gardens—
Indoors and Out**

Mimi Luebbermann

**Photographs by
Faith Echtermeyer**

CHRONICLE BOOKS
SAN FRANCISCO

Library of Congress Cataloging-in-Publication
data available.

ISBN: 0-8118-3553-7

Manufactured in China

Book design by Aufuldish & Warinner

Cover design by Lori Barra, TonBo designs

Distributed in Canada by Raincoast Books
9050 Shaughnessy Street
Vancouver, British Columbia V6P 6E5

10 9 8 7 6

Chronicle Books LLC
85 Second Street
San Francisco, California 94105

www.chroniclebooks.com

For Billy Cross and Michael James with
admiration, affection, and appreciation—
because orchids become you. F. E.

Contents

ORCHIDS TO GROW ON A WINDOWSILL   46

ORCHIDS TO GROW IN OUTDOOR CONTAINERS   66

ORCHIDS TO GROW IN THE GROUND   80

EXOTIC ORCHIDS   86

INTRODUCTION

Exotic, romantic, aloof in reputation, always admired in bloom, orchids are the prima donnas of the flower world. Orchids hypnotize. The color, fragrance, shape, and beauty of their flowers dazzle. An orchid in bloom transforms any room into a tropical palace. Truly, of all the flowering plants in the world, none seem so seductively alluring as the orchid family. ¶ Bewitched orchid fanciers accept their enslaved state with delighted stoicism. Swearing never again, they tote home "just one more" regardless of overcrowded windowsills or porches. What begins as a casual couple of orchids to perk up a dreary winter soon results in a collection flowing from the kitchen to the bedrooms, to the basement turned into an orchid habitat with timed lights, and to the sun-room remodeled as an expanded greenhouse. ¶ Those who admire, desire, but restrain themselves because they think that orchids are too tender, too technically difficult, and too fastidiously fussy, really need not resist. Many types of orchids have the knack of

A Cautionary Note
Even though samples of most of the wild orchids of the world have been collected and catalogued by scientists over the last four hundred years, there are new species being discovered every year. Sadly, the clearing of jungles, savannas, and large tracts of forestland has relentlessly encroached on native habitats, curtailing opportunities to discover still-unknown species. Those orchids that survive in the wild are endangered by commercial collectors who show little regard for continued regeneration. ¶ To protect the remaining native plantings, buy your plants from reputable growers and distributors who are themselves propagating the species or selling only propagated specimens, not collecting from the wild. Should you be so fortunate as to stumble across wild orchids, view them with awe but leave them undisturbed. Rarely, if ever, are wild orchids successfully transplanted.

casual survival on rock faces, in tree crotches, or in the thick duff of forest floors, and by mimicking their natural growing places, you will be rewarded with blooms in your living room as bright as those in their native habitat.

¶ If you succumb to orchid mania, console yourself with the knowledge that orchid collecting has been in vogue for the last two thousand plus years. Indeed, historical mention in Chinese and Japanese lore suggests people were tending orchids even four thousand years ago. In the third century B.C., the Greek philosopher Theophrastus wrote a book called Enquiry into Plants, in which he describes the family of orchids, so named because the twin fleshy underground bulbs bore a similarity to testicles (orchis, in Greek). This human association brought orchids some distinction, because prevailing medical wisdom held that plants mashed into pastes or stirred into tinctures cured the human parts they resembled. Orchid bulbs were ground up and prescribed as an aphrodisiac. This was the beginning of European fascination with orchids.

¶ Native European orchids stirred a medicinal interest, but aesthetically they paled in comparison to tropical species. It was the discovery of the fabulous orchids that grow around the equator that set off orchid-collecting hysteria in Europe. In the mid-sixteenth century, naturalists accompanying the European "discoverers" looking for gold and spices tramped through far-off jungles and across mountains, literally stumbling across flowers more exotic than had ever before been seen in Europe. Orchids from those lush tropical forests spent the trip to European ports deep in the black hold of a sailing ship, tossing and rolling over stormy waves. When they were unloaded in Europe, no one knew how to take care of them, and in the beginning, many, if not most of them, perished. Regardless, the hunt was on.

¶ Plants were gathered afar and brought back sometimes only as dried specimens or illustrations, and sometimes actually in bloom. Like ripples on a pond, the stir went further than the scientific world. The aristocracy and the newly rich industrialists became competitively entranced with orchids, setting off a demand for importation. Cattleya orchids played a major part in this early fascination. They came into England as packing for other tropical plants. William Cattley realized the stuff was actually plant material and out of curiosity nurtured it to foliage and blossom.

When the orchid, soon named after him, bloomed in 1818, it transfixed the horticultural world. By the nineteenth century, Europe was riveted to the spectacle of orchid collecting, importing, and auctioning.

¶ Tropical orchids would never have survived in the cold and wet European climate had their discovery not coincided with the invention of an industrial process to produce glass in thin sheets. Old-fashioned brick orangeries, built to protect citrus fruits, were expanded to large glass conservatories filled with orchids. Rabid in their desire to collect more of the exotic beauties, the most fanatical collectors engaged the services of professional orchid hunters, who cut down whole trees to collect plants living in the tops of them and ruthlessly stripped entire populations of native specimens to send back to their patrons. As the competition grew, some hunters obscured the location of their collecting sites, providing confusing or purposely incorrect information to throw other hunters off their trail. Some of the greedier drove up the price of orchids by purposely destroying plants in the wild so that their collected specimens, now rare, sold for increased sums at the orchid auctions.

¶ Many species shipped to Europe perished during the passage and many more later died in greenhouses until appropriate cultivation techniques were discovered. The rarity value started to diminish only as more horticulturists learned how to propagate orchids, and as imports of the sturdy, cooler-climate, highland orchids increased. Gradually, orchid mania died down, prices stabilized, and cultivation techniques became more certain. Still, it took years for orchidists to sort through all the misinformation this era produced and to catalogue correctly orchids and the location of their native habitats. A number of orchids were so overcollected during this time that they are rarely found in their native habitat.

¶ I began growing orchids out of a fascination with the serene beauty of their blooms, but I think the stage was set by earlier experiences. When I was a small child living in Virginia I went on a shopping trip with my father. He suddenly pulled over to the side of the road and stopped. He had caught sight of a little clearing dappled with sunlight in the middle of the woods. There were pink blooms dotting the green grass, probably Cypripedium acaule, pink lady's slipper orchids. I must have squatted down, for I remember viewing the orchids closely, admiring the crinkled surface of the slipper. My father was reverent in his appreciation, and now I know why. I never saw such a sight again in my childhood.

¶ The next time I encountered orchids was while living in Australia. On

the advice of some friendly folks at a lunch counter southwest of Perth, I wandered out into a sandy field to look for native orchids. In ignorance, I supposed them to be the size of cymbidiums, and not until I got down on my hands and knees did I discover the incredible beauty of the miniature native species orchids. I crawled on my knees for yards, marveling at the variety and abundance of the jewel-like blossoms.

¶ As a young gardener, I was irresistibly drawn to the exotic nature of orchids, but although I could nurture them while in bloom, I was frustrated with the care of them throughout the following nonbloom period, never knowing when to water, when to fertilize, or which window to set them in. Alas, they didn't rebloom for me, and for years I gave up in despair, sure that I hadn't the knack. Reading Rex Stout's mystery novels about the orchid-growing detective Nero Wolfe, who employed a full-time gardener and filled three greenhouses with blooms, made me all the more despondent.

¶ Now, I realize that successful orchid growing depends upon choosing varieties with growing requirements you can duplicate in your own home, necessitating the only rule of starting with orchids: If you can't grow it, don't buy it! The first step in building your orchid-growing confidence is to control the undisciplined buying of just any intriguing orchid.

¶ *Even as I understand the wisdom of such judicious choosing, I admit the beauty of orchids is so captivating that I have a hard time reining in my enthusiasm. Their beauty calls out, and before you know it, homeward bound is a cultivar with fussy requirements for humidity, heat, and light that your house cannot provide. My suggestion, if you break the rule (and I often do), is to enjoy these picky types while they bloom, and when the bloom finishes give them away to an orchid society, return them to the breeder, or donate them to a botanical garden. Without the right growing conditions, they will never rebloom and may even perish.*

¶ *The orchids pictured in this book live comfortably in our living environment. Armed with a few cultivation rules, you can make your windowsills, fire escapes, and porches glow with the singular beauty of orchids. The selection of so few orchid varieties from so many (how to choose from thirty thousand plus varieties?) was made according to ease of cultivation, general availability, and the beauty of a plant's blossom or sweetness of its fragrance, obviously a point of personal prejudice. Practicing with these species will prepare you for caring for the types you discover you prefer.*

¶ *This book has been designed for the beginner orchid grower. It doesn't require you to wade through talk about footcandles of light or other technical jargon impossible to sort out when you are just creeping shyly into the world of orchids. Learning how to pronounce the Latin names is hard enough, plus restraining your impulse to buy whichever and all orchids you meet. Starting slowly by buying orchids with the highest likelihood of success in an everyday home environment, not in a greenhouse and not under artificial lights, and working simply to provide a healthy environment is sufficient when you are getting going. Later, as you gain experience, you will appreciate the wealth of technical information available in other books and resources.*

¶ *My job has been to pare down the information so the new orchid fancier is not overwhelmed and quits before starting, but has the essential knowledge necessary for initial success. Once you've experienced the pleasure of watching the buds on a flower stalk fatten and burst into blossom, I know, from that moment on, the artful persuasion of orchids themselves will carry the day.*

CHARACTERISTICS OF ORCHIDS

The old-fashioned description of sickly people as "delicate as a hothouse orchid" has left the orchid family languishing through the years with the reputation of needing to be cosseted in greenhouses with professional orchid doctors hovering worriedly. Fussy varieties from tropical countries with days that fairly drip with humidity do indeed require a delicate balance of moisture, light, and daytime and nighttime temperature levels to continue to grow and bloom outside of their native environment. But with orchids growing in every corner of the world except the most frozen climes, varieties suited for home windowsills and gardens abound.

¶ The most difficult aspect of orchid cultivation is grasping the complexity of the orchid family. Forming the largest plant family on earth, orchid species are estimated to number twenty-five thousand, and because orchids cross-pollinate so easily, horticulturists have created additional thousands of hybrid as well as intergeneric varieties (crosses of two different genera). Unwinding the family genealogy is less important to the novitiate in the beginning than is focusing on unfickle performers to fill the house with year-round orchid bloom. Yet parentage affects growth characteristics. Some *dendrobiums* grow so large they overtake a neatly organized windowsill, while other types with one different parent stay small and manageable. Members of the same orchid group may require completely different cultivation techniques to bring them into bloom.

¶ Taking time to understand the naming of the plants can add to your success. Both size and cultural requirements are genetically inherited, so if you know the complete names of your orchids you will be able to learn exactly what you can expect from your plants. Keep in mind that species orchids differ greatly from hybrid varieties with the same name—you may have heard *phalaenopsis* are easy to grow, but make sure you choose the more vigorous *phalaenopsis* hybrids, not the species varieties. Also be aware that a plant labeled *Dendrobium phalaenopsis* is a *dendrobium*. Here the word *phalaenopsis*, meaning mothlike, describes the bloom shape and doesn't claim a family relationship.

¶ Orchid names usually are given in Latin—the first, or genus, name followed by the species name and then the variety or clonal name, for example, *Paphiopedilum armeniacum* 'Jessie.' Sometimes the second name describes the plant, its color or place of origin, or the person for whom the plant was named (such as *Cattleya skinneri*, a *cattleya* named after Mr. George Skinner). Names also indicate crossbreeding: A *Brassolaeliocattleya* orchid has species of *brassavola*, *cattleya*, and *laelia* in its ancestry. Orchid pros rattle off abbreviations, calling *phalaenopsis* "phals," *paphiopedilums* "paphs," and crosses of *brassia*, *laelia*, and *cattleya* as "Blc's"—all quite daunting when you are just starting in the world of orchids. To further complicate matters, hybrids carry the initials of their awards. "AOS" means the American Orchid Society has awarded that plant a prize for its superior characteristics. Take your time and, when confused, ask. Pretty soon, you will be spouting off the orchid lingo with the best of the experts.

¶ A starting place to learn about orchids is in the distinction in their growth patterns. Orchids grow in two different ways. *Sympodial* orchids, such as *dendrobiums* and *cymbidiums*, produce new growth from the base of the plant, rather than from the tip of existing stems. They often have pseudobulbs to help them through periods of dormancy or drought. Like a true bulb, such as a narcissus, a pseudobulb absorbs and stores water and nutrients, but it is actually a thickened stem. *Sympodial* orchids can be either ever-green or deciduous.

¶ *Monopodial* orchids, such as *vandas* and *phalaenopsis,* have a main stem that grows upward, year after year. Leaves come out alternately from each side of the stem. *Monopodial* orchids do not have pseudobulbs and consequently have no means of stor-ing water. These are completely dependent on their immediate environment for water and nourishment. *Monopodials* are always evergreen.

¶ Some orchids scale tree trunks or rock faces in their native habitat to bring them up closer to the light. Some of these, whether *monopodial* or *sympodial,* cannot be contained easily in pots and prefer to grow on a cork bark raft—a flat, vertical surface that sup-ports their climb upward.

¶ The roots of orchids differ according to their native habitat. Terrestrial orchids grow in the ground, sometimes with tubers, rhizomes, or pseudobulbs to nourish them through dormant periods or dry seasons. Some types of terrestrial orchids are decidu-ous and some evergreen. Terrestrial varieties are accustomed to having their roots buried, so they don't require the coarse potting mix provided by orchid bark, but to keep the roots from rotting they need a loose, quickly draining soil.

¶ The orchids that drape themselves exotically in trees are known as *epiphytes* or, if over rocks, *lithophytes.* These cohabit nonparasitically with the trees or rocks that support them, drawing their nutriments from water that falls upon their roots and from decom-posing organic matter that often builds up around the roots. The exposed roots look whitish or grayish, and the outer cover, called velamen, soaks up water as effectively as a sponge. The tough stringy interior gives the roots limpetlike strength to hang on to their

perches. Usually these varieties are evergreen, and most of them live in humid places where rainfall occurs regularly. However, they often must be able to withstand dry periods in their native habitats, so many of these varieties prefer to dry out between waterings. The potting mix for *epiphytes* needs to be a loose one with large air spaces between the particles so that the orchid roots are exposed, as in their native habitat.

¶ Different orchid types need different levels of light to grow and bloom; being so widely distributed over the world, orchids grow in many different circumstances. They stand out in sunny meadows, hang off trees, or root in the ground in deep shade or in the dappled sunlight of forests. Some take advantage of early spring sunshine and bloom before the trees they live in leaf out, remaining dormant during the rest of the season. Many terrestrials have a long dormant period, when they rest underground.

¶ Knowing the light needs of your orchid and placing it in an appropriate place in your house or garden are critical for keeping it healthy and bringing it back into bloom. Some plants such as the forest floor–dwelling *paphiopedilums* require bright light, but should direct sunlight hit the tender, succulent leaves, they will sunburn as surely as tender, winter-white skin crisps in tropical sunshine. By contrast, *cattleyas* have leathery leaves to withstand all but the hottest, burning sun.

¶ Appraising the light that falls through your windows can be trickier than you would imagine, for even wintry sunshine burns through south-facing windows, while summer light through a north-facing window may be bright but will not be bright enough to cast a shadow. Finding just the right spot is the key, because if orchids are deprived of the light they need, they will not bloom.

¶ Humidity is another requirement of orchids. You can imagine that tropical orchids used to the high humidity in tropical jungles and rain forests are unhappy transplanted to our central-heated houses, with their dry heat. Still, humidity is easily provided by placing the plant on a gravel-filled tray or saucer topped with water. The plant container sits on top of the gravel, and the evaporating moisture provides humidity. It is important that the base of the container not be submerged in water; the water will wick up and saturate the potting mix, and for most orchids, the too-constant moisture will cause root rot and plant death. Orchids that live in arid mountains or in other low-humidity locations do not need the kind of humidity that tropical orchids require. These orchids thrive like the most ordinary plants, with just elemental attention to water and nutrients.

¶ Orchids grow very slowly, and consequently they need less nutrition than many other plants. In the wild, they draw nutrients from decomposing organic material and from the rain. In pots indoors, they dwell in a sterile soil or bark medium, and therefore you must fertilize them regularly. Plants have a growing season, usually corresponding to spring and summer, when they need nitrogen to help manufacture leaves. During the dormant season, generally winter, when the plants rest and growth slows almost to a halt, less nutrition is needed. But different orchids bloom, grow, and rest at different times, so it's important to follow their natural cycles. For the beginner with a mixed collection, the best method is to fertilize every two weeks with a diluted solution of high-nitrogen fertilizer.

¶ The variety of bloom in the orchid family is incredible. The genetic proliferation comes from orchids' ingenuity in enticing bees, flies, moths, ants, or even hummingbirds to enter the flowers and carry away pollen, usually unknowingly, to fertilize other blossoms. Some orchids resemble traps, luring in pollinating creatures by exuding sticky nectar or enticing fragrances. Other blooms resemble the pollinator's natural mate, convincingly inviting it to couple, but really only ensnaring it to cover it with pollen. The variety of orchid bloom is like the results of a fabulously complex design challenge: How many ways can the same basic flower parts—three flower petals, three sepals, and a column that holds the stamens and pistils—be altered to entice a species-specific pollinator? Although its multitude of pollination strategies has given the orchid family resilience throughout its long evolutionary past, with the modern destruction of habitat and consequent death of whole species of insects and birds, the survival of many orchid species is threatened. Once a butterfly species dies out, the orchid dependent on its pollinating chores perishes as well.

¶ Remembering that orchids grow slowly reminds you to be patient, to give each plant time, and to measure its bloom success in years, not months. With these strictures and some guidance, you can be assured of blooms from orchids all year long, cheering the dismal days of winter and festooning the outdoor garden during the summer months.

About growing orchids

In their native habitats, orchids grow as wildly and neglected as weeds. The traveler to tropical orchid-growing countries can hardly believe the care-less ease of local gardeners, whose huge, floriferous orchid plants have a garden role as humble as our geraniums or pansies. Those of us who live in climates less appealing to orchids struggle to satisfy artificially what is normally casually provided.

¶ Orchids grow easily when they have their cultural requirements met, but because orchids originate from many different parts of the world, their needs vary enormously from variety to variety. Calling a plant homesick works well as a reminder: A plant will sicken if transplanted to a foreign environment, as much as a child wilts when strangers fill in for parents, not knowing just how to slice a peanut butter and jelly sandwich (sideways or crossways—get it wrong and there could be hysterics!).

¶ Imitating your transplanted orchid's natural climate and diet encourages your plant to prosper. The important elements of home care are water, humidity, temperature, pot-ting mix, fertilizer, and light level. This list of requirements is much the same for any houseplant, and with practice and blooming successes (as well as mourned plant losses), you learn how to make your orchids feel truly at home.

WATER

Water carries nutrients from the soil or potting mix up through the roots and stem to the leaves and flowers. As it evaporates through pores in the leaves in a process called transpiration, the roots draw up more water, like straws sucking up liquid. Terrestrial, or ground-dwelling, orchids like a loose soil with lots of compost for good drainage, for, like bulbs, they quickly rot if left soggy over a period of time. *Epiphytic* orchids grow fastened to trunks of trees with their roots hanging out in the air, so that they can suck in water quickly during light, misty rains or seasonal tropical downpours. In pots, *epiphytic* orchids need a loose bark mixture that allows large air spaces around the roots to keep the roots healthy.

¶ Some types of orchids have developed thickened stems, called pseudobulbs, to store water and nutrients for the extended dry seasons between tropical downpours. Other orchids have roots that can absorb the water they need out of humid air. Know your orchids' needs, and be prepared to water specifically to each variety's requirements. Many orchid lovers use a simple system of colored tags or dots on labels to indicate watering once a week, twice a week, or daily. Above all, don't overwater orchids, especially not *cattleyas*, which prefer to dry out between waterings.

¶ During periods of high evaporation, such as hot or windy days, the rate of water loss from the leaves increases, so the roots need more water. When the leaves lose more water than the roots can quickly replenish, the plant wilts. During hot and windy days, make sure to increase your watering. Misting the leaves also improves water absorption in hot weather, slowing transpiration from the leaves. During winter months, when most orchids are growing slowly, water less frequently.

¶ Healthy roots that are in a growing phase have bright green tips; the rest of the year the roots should be white and firm to the touch. As the plants age, some of their roots die naturally, but red-flag any plant with unhealthy, shriveling leaves and few, if any, healthy roots. In most cases, your overwatering will have caused the problem.

¶ It's not easy to prescribe a formula for watering because during different seasons the amount of water a plant needs changes. During cold, rainy, damp weather, moisture stays in the mix longer, the plants absorb less water because they are growing more slowly in the cold temperature, and there is less transpiration from the leaves. You must water less at such times.

¶ In warm weather, the plants are growing and so they need more water to manufacture roots, leaves, and blooms. At the same time, warm temperatures cause an increase in the amount of water transpiring off the leaves, so the plant must adjust and absorb more water than during cold weather. Hot, dry weather draws water out of the potting mix as well as increases the amount of water a plant requires. More frequent watering and misting will help a plant make it through hot summer temperatures without stress.

¶ The type and size of the pot and the plant size also affect watering schedules. Plastic and glazed ceramic pots keep potting mix wet longer. Mix in unglazed ceramic pots dries out quicker; the moisture evaporates through the sides. Large plants will absorb water faster than small plants, but larger pots compensate for this difference. Cork bark rafts dry out quickly and must be watered daily, twice daily in hot weather. Generally, keep plants with roots that prefer never to dry out, such as *paphiopedilums*, in plastic pots or glazed ceramic pots. *Cattleyas* like their roots dry between waterings, so keep these in unglazed pots to help the mix to dry out.

¶ Water your orchids overhead; when they are in bloom, avoid splashing the blossoms. Water drained off should never be reused on other plants, to avoid spreading diseases.

Watering thoroughly disperses any buildup of fertilizer salts, which is important because too much fertilizer can burn tender orchid roots.

¶ When you are starting out with orchids, try watering once a week consistently. Set a specific day during the week when you plan to water your orchids; a reliable watering habit will start off your orchids successfully. Place the orchids in a sink or outside in clement weather and water generously with a hose or spray attachment, letting the water flush through the mix at least three times for each orchid. During the warm days of spring and summer, increase your watering to two days a week. Water early in the morning so the plant can dry off by evening. Damp plants in cool evening temperatures can develop crown rot or fungal diseases. Do not let water sit in folds of the orchid plant or inside the blooms.

¶ Correctly watering plants in containers is always a little difficult, but because orchid roots are so moisture sensitive, watering your orchids becomes a life-or-death matter much more quickly than with other types of plants. Leave an orchid plant in a glass jar filled with water for a day and you will see the velamen start to peel off and rot away. One grower with years of experience suggests keeping a potted container *without* a plant amongst your collection. Turn out the container before you water to check how dry the mix has become below the surface. When in doubt, dig your finger down into the mix to check the moisture level. If a plant begins to look really unhealthy—leaves are shriveling, changing color, or drooping—turn it out and check the roots. Mushy, rotting roots most probably mean you are overwatering. Shriveling leaves and roots that look dark and dried-up indicate you need to increase your watering.

¶ Practice lifting orchid containers before you water them. With time, you will find you can judge whether the plant needs to be watered by the weight of the container, useful during flashes of intense summer heat or a cold, wet spring. You may lose some plants until you get the knack of judging when your plants need water. Consider these losses somewhat like cookies you burned when you first tried baking and simply adjust your habits and check up sooner.

HUMIDITY

Some types of orchids need high humidity to flourish, but the ones suggested in this book are usually satisfied with humidity levels found in the home. However, in wintertime, home heating systems notoriously dry out the air, and in summer extreme temperatures may call for misting, so planning ways to maintain humidity for your orchids is essential.

¶ Keeping your orchids together on a bench or a shelf increases humidity naturally. You can also rest the container on top of a saucer filled with gravel and water. The gravel keeps the bottom of the container elevated out of the water, and the evaporation of the water increases humidity around the plant. Orchid catalogues and specialty stores also offer large plastic trays with grids to elevate the plants over a water reservoir, a system that makes watering easier and raises humidity levels.

¶ Misting daily with a squirt bottle also keeps the humidity level up, and for *epiphytic* plants mounted on bark, provides additional water to the roots. Make sure to mist in the early morning so that the plant foliage will have time to dry out before evening—a preventative step against possible fungal diseases and crown rot.

TEMPERATURE

Some orchids grow in steamy, sauna-hot jungles, thousands of feet high on cool, temperate mountains, or in a cool temperature situation next to waterfalls with a constant supply of misty droplets in the air. Transplanting an orchid to your home means you must provide temperatures within the range that the plant comfortably grows. Commercial growers categorize orchids by their temperature needs: cool types from mountain growing regions, intermediate types that grow in temperatures between 50 and 90°F, and hot types that like a real tropical environment.

¶ Temperature affects bloom as well as the health of the plant. *Cymbidiums* need a cool autumn to trigger the production of bloom stalks. Buying a maximum/minimum thermometer will help you find out the temperature ranges in the rooms you plan to use for growing orchids. Most of the orchids mentioned in this book need the intermediate temperatures most commonly found in homes. Double-check the temperature requirements of your orchids, especially the temperature that triggers bloom formation.

¶ Most orchids benefit from a vacation outside during the summer months. When you move your orchids out, remember their leaves are as winter-tender as tourists' skin when first exposed to summer sun, and start them in the shade to get them used to the stronger light levels. Sunburn on leaves looks like leathery brown spots. Gradually move your plants to a location where they receive dappled sunshine throughout the day, but no noonday sun. If a heat wave starts to send the temperature soaring, compensate with watering and misting several times a day.

POTTING MIXES

Orchid potting mixes are somewhat like menswear: You can buy premixed varieties off the rack, so to speak, or you can try to tailor your own. In the beginning, if you think your orchid needs repotting, you may be puzzled about just what to buy. Almost all orchid growers have a special mix they tout as the most successful medium for orchids, but be forewarned that no single mix suits all orchid types.

¶ Examine the medium your orchid was originally potted in, and request the same grade from your professional orchid grower or nursery, taking into account that an old medium may have disintegrated if it has been some years since repotting. What is most important for the health of the orchid is the size of the individual pieces in the mix. As a general rule, experts suggest that the larger the root diameter, the coarser the mix should be. Coarse roots in a fine grade will soon rot, unable to get sufficient oxygen from the tiny spaces between the fine particles. Fine roots in a coarse grade will dry up, exposed to too much air in the mix and unable to make contact with the moisture absorbed by the large pieces of bark. Make sure to buy mixes that specify they are formulated for orchids to guarantee that the mix has been sterilized, a safeguard against viral and fungal diseases.

¶ Most of the bark used in mixes for container-grown orchids is sterilized fir bark. This bark, as it breaks down, does not contribute any nutrition to the orchid plant, which is why you must fertilize your orchids. Another component of orchid mixes is lava rock, which absorbs water, keeping the mix damp longer. As the bark decomposes to a finer material, the larger rock pieces, which don't break down, will maintain the air spaces in the mix that the orchid roots need. Having lava rock in your mix allows you to leave the orchid plant undisturbed for a little longer, without fearing the roots will rot from lack of oxygen. Some orchids do not like to be repotted, and a mix with rocks gives you another year before disturbing them.

¶ Many catalogues offer orchid growing mediums, and after trying some of them, you can begin to devise your own. Unless your orchid begins to look unhealthy, let it live in a medium for at least a year before you judge its success.

CORK BARK RAFTS

Some *epiphytic* orchids prefer to have their roots exposed to the air. These grow best on slabs of cork bark, often called rafts, available in different sizes to suit the size of your plant. Rafts also allow *epiphytes* to grow easily in their natural hanging form and to grow quickly, unrestrained by pot size. Tie plants gently to the bark with nylon fishing line. Most *epiphytes* need a thin bedding of sphagnum moss to help trap a little moisture for their roots. Because they have no potting medium to retain moisture, water or mist them daily. During hot weather, mist two or three times a day.

PREPARED GROUND

Terrestrial orchids need a very loose soil with plenty of compost so that it drains well and the water never soggily surrounds the roots. Make sure to check the specific needs of the terrestrial orchid you are planting, but as a general rule, dig in generous quantities of compost.

¶ Prepare the soil two to three weeks before you set out your orchids. If the soil is so wet that it falls off the shovel in clumps, you will have to delay starting until the soil dries out somewhat or risk compacting the ground, making it rock hard. Compacted soil has less oxygen, and roots deprived of oxygen will not grow successfully.

¶ First remove existing plant material such as weeds or plants that you no longer want to grow there. Add 6 inches of organic compost, and with a shovel, a spade, or a machine such as a rototiller, turn over the soil to a depth of 12 to 18 inches. Water the turned soil and allow any undesirable seeds that may be in the ground to sprout over the next two weeks. When the ground is damp but not soggy, remove the newly sprouted weeds. Using a hoe or shovel, break up any clods and rake the surface smooth for planting.

FERTILIZERS

Because orchids in pots grow in sterile potting mix, you must provide the nutrients necessary for their growth. The major nutrients needed for plant growth are nitrogen, phosphorus, and potassium (N, P, K). Nutrient needs for nitrogen are greatest during periods of growth, typically spring and summer, so these are the best times to fertilize your orchids with a high-nitrogen fertilizer. Commercial fertilizers list their contents as the percentage of each nutrient, in the order nitrogen-phosphorus-potassium. For example, an NPK formula of 20-20-20 has equal amounts of nitrogen, phosphorus, and potassium. Most high-nitrogen orchid formulations are 30-10-10; the low-nitrogen ones are 10-30-30, or 0-10-10. They all come in the form of water-soluble pellets that you mix with water. Fertilize plants after you have watered them thoroughly; the wet potting mix helps minimize the possibility of fertilizer damage to the roots.

¶ Watch for buildup of salts, a condition that can occur when plants are overfertilized or when watering practices do not flush out excess fertilizer. Look for a whitish crust on the plant's roots or the inside of the container. To eliminate salt buildup, decrease the amount you are fertilizing and water plants thoroughly between fertilizing. Organic fertilizers such as fish emulsion and kelp formulas do not contain the salts, and although some growers object to their odoriferousness, others find the plants benefit from applications of organic fertilizers.

¶ There is a great deal of controversy about the best way to fertilize orchids. Many books call for changing formulas; many growers suggest a year-round schedule of a 20-20-20 formula. For success as well as simplicity, follow the recommendation of an experienced and practical orchid grower. He uses a pelleted orchid fertilizer with a 30-10-10 formula diluted half-strength to fertilize his mixed collection of orchids every two weeks, throughout the year. He says orchids absorb the nutrients they need in the proper proportions, as long as they are fed regularly and not overfed with too strong a solution. (There are just a few exceptions, but these are noted specifically under the individual growing instructions.) This simple system will make it easy for you to keep to a schedule, and your orchids will prosper. Later in your orchid-growing career, you can try the more complicated seasonal changing of formulas if you choose.

RESTING PERIOD

Some plants, after they have bloomed or just before they bloom, enter a period of resting. At this time, you need to reduce watering and feeding. These resting periods relate to the climate conditions of the orchid's homeland, which may have an annual dry period between rainy seasons. Just as bears must hibernate, regardless of whether they are

living in Hawaii or Vermont, in the wilds or in a zoo, your orchids need to continue to take a rest according to their native patterns. Make sure you follow their natural cycles.

LIGHT

Ensuring your plant gets enough light is essential for blooming, but there's no general prescription that works for all orchids. Orchids need varying amounts of light, depending on their native cultural conditions. There is an Australian orchid that grows and blooms underground, needing no light at all. Orchids accustomed to living on the jungle floor will sunburn if placed in a sunny window. *Cattleyas* are the sun lovers, and you see them suspended high up in greenhouses, soaking in the rays. Your windows provide different light levels depending upon their aspect. South-facing windows catch direct sunlight during winter and bright, but not direct, sunlight during the summer. North-facing windows provide diffuse light, no direct sunshine, and generally too little light for most orchids. East- and west-facing windows give direct morning and afternoon sunlight, respectively. West-facing windows, even in winter months, can be too blazing hot for some orchids, and you may need to provide a thin curtain to protect the orchids. A thin, gauzy curtain can cut out direct sunshine while still allowing light in. Alternatively, you can position thin, translucent sheets of rice paper to shield delicate orchids from direct sunlight.

¶ Some growers, as they become more confident and build up their collections, turn closets or basements into orchid gardens by installing artificial lights. If you run out of room for your orchids, having filled every available windowsill, bookcase, tabletop, and kitchen counter, this may be an option you wish to research further. Other possibilities are greenhouse windows or small greenhouses.

REPOTTING

When you start your orchid collection, you don't think about repotting, but before long the plants seem to be overfilling their pots, hanging off the sides in an ungainly fashion and with more roots outside than inside. Mature plants that you purchase from a nursery may already be due for a repotting if the roots encircle the container several times. Even tidy plants with plenty of root space will need repotting if the once-coarse potting mix begins to resemble well-aged compost.

¶ The correct timing of repotting is critical; repot at the wrong time and your orchid may not rebloom for the next year. In most cases, orchids should be repotted just after blooming. With *phalaenopsis*, plants should not be repotted until the root tips turn bright green after a bloom phase, signaling the beginning of a root growth period. Learn the specific time to repot each variety of your orchids. If you are not sure, a good rule is to repot when new growth appears, or when tips of roots turn green.

¶ Match the grade of potting mix to the size of your orchid's roots, choosing a fine grade for an orchid with small, thin roots, medium grade for medium-size roots, and a coarse grade for thick roots. Soak the chosen mix for at least four hours before using. Make sure your plant fits its new container. When it is centered inside the empty container, the roots should hang down inside without cramping or doubling up, with about 1 or 2 inches of extra space around the inside of the pot. *Dendrobium* roots like cramped spaces, so their pots can be smaller. *Epiphytic* orchids are the exception;

because their roots are often exposed to the air in their native habitat, you may leave some roots hanging over the edge of the container if you cannot fit them all in when you repot.

¶ Push the plant out of its original container. Gently strip off the old bark pieces, even those clinging to the roots, though being careful not to damage the roots. Examine the roots carefully, and with your clippers, cut off any blackened, hollow, or rotted roots. Note the condition of the roots, for they tell you a great deal about your watering practices. Dried-up roots indicate the roots have not gotten enough water; rotted roots probably indicate overwatering. Fungal and viral diseases can be spread from plant to plant through clipper blades. When you are repotting several plants, it is a good idea to disinfect the clippers after you trim one plant and before you start on the next. Pass the blades through a gas flame until they are too hot to touch, or immerse them in bleach.

¶ Holding the plant upright inside the container, add the potting mix, tamping down around the edge of the container to firm the mix around the roots without injuring them. Continue to add mix, leaving a 1-inch space at the top of the container for watering. Pseudobulbs should rest above the surface of the potting mix, for buried pseudobulbs tend to rot. Water the plant well.

¶ After repotting, staking is critical to the plant's recovery. Orchids do not like to wobble in their containers, so provide support until the roots develop to steady the plant. Tie the plant to a thin bamboo stake, or alternatively, use a handmade or purchased rhizome clip to brace the plant. Some orchid raisers shape the metal wire clip so it hooks to the side of the container and across the roots. Others shape it into a T—the vertical part goes down into the container, the horizontal part across the top of the roots, firmly securing them. Once you have a model, you will find it simple to make clips yourself with heavy wire and a set of needle-nose pliers.

¶ Water thoroughly after repotting. Then, limit direct watering, but begin misting twice a day. Watch for new roots or new growth to develop. Once you see new growth, resume the plant's regular watering and fertilizing schedule. Make sure to note the date you repotted the plant on the back of the label. Lead pencil stays readable most reliably.

DIVISIONS AND KEIKIS

Some of the big clump-forming orchids will eventually outgrow even the biggest pots. The best time to divide them is when new growth has just started. Prize the plant apart into groups of at least three pseudobulbs and repot each group into a fresh container; smaller groups will take longer to come back into bloom. It may be three years before the youngest pseudobulbs bloom. The largest should flower next year. Some types of orchids, such as *dendrobiums*, form plantlets, called keikis, along a main stem. Once the keikis roots have grown about 1 inch, you can prize the plantlets off the stem and pot them. Before you begin to break up a plant, check with a professional that it needs to be divided and inquire about the proper season and procedure for the specific variety.

HARDINESS

Hardy and *tender* are two words tossed around by gardeners that roughly distinguish how well a plant withstands cold. Tender plants freeze to death in cold temperatures.

Hardy plants stand up to the cold or at least a certain amount of it. Plants are often described as hardy to a specific temperature—"hardy to 32°F," for example. Half-hardy plants usually survive a cold spell, but may not survive extended cold periods. Most of the orchids we grow come from tropical areas; they die when the temperature drops much below 40°F. Some nontropical orchids need a period of cool evenings to set off the signals to form bloom stalks; others, such as *Bletilla striata*, don't mind snow all winter as long as they have a good bed of mulch and compost on top of them. Make sure you understand the hardiness of your orchids.

PESTS

Outdoors, in moist climates, slugs and snails can become very persistent in the spring or fall, and their ravenous appetites may quickly ruin blossoms you have anticipated for a year. Maintain a vigilant watch in the evening with a flashlight, and hand-pick any slugs and snails off the plants into a bag that you can tie tightly and discard into the garbage. A strip of copper wound tightly around the base of containers creates a barrier against slugs and snails; it gives them a slight shock, which keeps them from clambering up the sides of the container to devour your blooms. Snail baits are also effective in deterring these destructive pests.

¶ Rodents love pseudobulbs, and if you notice any nibbles, they may be the culprit. Bait, standard traps, or live traps such as Havaheart are the only ways to protect your plants.

¶ Orchids are susceptible to a number of different insect problems, indoors and out. The new, tender growth is particularly susceptible, so watch closely in spring when

plants are beginning to put out tender growth. Look at your plants each time you water them, for early detection will help you keep the problems under control before the plant becomes too weakened. Soft-bodied aphids, and scale, which resemble warts, are problems you can easily identify. Use organic "safer soaps" to destroy them, or gently wipe the plants with a soft cloth dipped into rubbing alcohol. Impossible to see with the human eye are the microscopic spider mites and thrips that leave the underside of the leaves looking strangely whitish. Watch the leaves of your orchids particularly during drier seasons, such as when you are reducing water or misting while the plant is resting. Increase humidity, wash the leaves daily, and use an organic "safer soap" to destroy the pests. Make sure to isolate the plant from your orchid collection until the problem is under control.

¶ After you bring your plants back indoors from summering outside, you may find they suddenly become infested with insects that are hatching out in the warmer indoor environment. Watch for them carefully and treat immediately.

DISEASES

Orchids can be infected with viral diseases through bad growing practices. Professional growers never reuse any potting mix, discarding all of it and repotting into new mix. Usually viral diseases show up as distorted plant parts and blooms, variegated color, and streaking in the leaves. Don't confuse viral symptoms with the accordion-pleating in leaves that's caused by irregular watering.

BLOOMING

Having an orchid rebloom for you is an indescribable pleasure that combines pure satisfaction, one-hundred-percent smug self-congratulation, and awestruck humiliation that you should be so lucky. When the buds start to color up and fatten just before they are ready to open, do not shift the position of the orchid—the blooms will twist awkwardly trying to face the light. To prolong the bloom, withhold fertilizer and keep the plant in a cool room out of direct sunlight.

¶ Make sure you stake the bloom carefully so its weight does not cause the stalk to break. Set a piece of bamboo, an attractive bit of tree branch, or some curly willow deep into the pot. Carefully tie the stalk to the support in several places with raffia or florists wire twists to support the blooms. After bloom, check the variety to learn whether you should cut off the stalk at the base or trim it back to another node so that it reblooms.

IF AT FIRST YOU DON'T SUCCEED

With orchids, you must persevere. Even the easiest orchids in the care of the most experienced breeders may take their time reblooming. Realize that orchids you bought in bloom from a nursery or breeder may take two years or more to adjust to your care and bloom again. Orchid growers, both professionals and aficionados, concede that orchids challenge their expertise by seductively withholding flowers during some years.

¶ Keep experimenting to find the varieties that grow and bloom most satisfactorily in your home, and then research other orchid species that grow under similar conditions to broaden your collection. Move a plant to a different location if it doesn't thrive.

Subtle differences of light, temperature, altitude, humidity, and care can induce a plant to bloom in one windowsill or location but not another. Join a local orchid club to get tips and advice. Find the nearest grower and attend any workshops or classes offered. Take your ailing plants to the orchid professional you purchased it from for a consultation.

¶ Most importantly, keep records of the orchids you buy, note their names, and research their parentage so you fully understand their growing needs. Record when your plants bloom, and how long the blossoms last. On the back of their parentage tags, keep track of when you repotted them so that you can gauge when you must repot again.

¶ Many orchid fanciers choose to maintain some orchids year-round on their windowsills while boarding out the more exacting types with professional growers who charge a small monthly fee. These professional services offer regulated greenhouses to care for your orchids, returning your plants when they start to bloom again. Consider this option if you long to collect varieties of orchids with cultural conditions difficult to provide in your home.

¶ When your desire to expand your orchid collection becomes thwarted by limited growing space, you may find yourself moving into the more advanced stage of growing orchids under lights or investing in a small—but it should be expandable—greenhouse. At this point you are well launched into a pastime that promises you years of relaxing study of plant habitats all over the world from the comfort of your backyard. Enjoy your vocation and realize your skills protect and nurture some of the most beautiful plants on the planet.

ORCHIDS TO
GROW ON A
WINDOWSILL

Anyone visiting the house of an orchid lover can immediately identify someone head over heels in orchid fascination. The signals are clear: Every windowsill is filled with plants. Orchids in bloom are sprinkled around on the top of the piano and on chair-side tables or are dramatically gracing the entrance hall, many scenting the air with fragrance. Tiny orchids perched vertically on bark make you lean close to see their miniature forms. As you walk from room to room, if you are unfamiliar with the complexity and intricacy of the blossoms, you may find yourself silently promising to stop at the nearest florist on the way home. ?❦ Indeed, many people become windowsill growers with just such an introduction. Although buying one orchid on the spur of the moment rarely seems to presage a life overflowing with orchids, it often happens in such a casual fashion. In these modern times, one tray of orchids promises a simpler, gentler, peaceful life. Watching over your plants, you are rewarded with flowers jewel-like in their perfection. Bringing one plant back into bloom after a year, or with some of the varieties, after several months, is a splendid measure of accomplishment, plain for all to see. ?❦ Growing orchids on a windowsill is not difficult, as long as you rigorously confine your plant choices to those that prosper in the setting you can provide. Note carefully your window outlooks, the amount of direct sun that beats in, so you can match the amount of light to a plant's requirements. Plants that enjoy humidity must sit on gravel trays or saucers, and you must remember to mist them every morning. Watch the light change during the seasons and adjust your plants' positions accordingly. With water and nutrition, patience and perseverance, your plants will reward you with the highest compliment—blooms of greatest beauty.

BRASSAVOLA NODOSA, LADY OF THE NIGHT

The name "lady of the night" suggests a number of elegant things, none of which at first glance apply to this inconspicuous orchid with elongated leathery leaves. Yet, like the magical quality of fairy tales, the perfume of its flowers floats through the night air and transforms the ordinary into the exotic. The flowers look like bow-tie artworks gracing a Tiffany package, with long, swirling, thin petals in green or white frilling a heart-shaped lip. ¶ Grow this orchid on a cork bark raft, or in a ceramic pot with coarse bark and rocks and lots of room for its long, trailing roots. Water and feed lady of the night as you would a cattleya, letting it dry out between waterings. Watch for the new pseudobulbs to appear after it blooms, then increase watering for several months until they become full size. If you are growing lady of the night on a cork bark raft, make sure you mist regularly every day and more often during hot, dry summer days. If the bulbs begin to shrivel, water more frequently. ¶ **HOW TO DO IT** ¶ During the winter months, keep lady of the night on a south-, east-, or west-facing windowsill, where it will receive bright sun. The foliage should be light green, dark green indicating too little light. If you are growing this orchid in a pot, place it on gravel in a saucer filled with water. In the summer the plant benefits from placement outside in a lathhouse or a shady spot, but be sure to maintain a high humidity by misting the cork raft regularly or keeping the pot saucer filled with water. Water a potted plant once a week, twice a week during a summer heat spell, and twice a week while the pseudobulbs are growing. Feed it every two weeks with a 30-10-10 orchid fertilizer diluted half-strength according to the directions on the container. Use a cork bark raft with a bedding of sphagnum moss or fill a pot with coarse-grade orchid bark mix and repot after two years or when the mix has broken down to a fine texture.

Lady of the Night
Brassavola nodosa

What You Need
30-10-10 orchid fertilizer,
diluted half-strength

When to Buy
In bloom

Light
Morning or afternoon sun during
winter months
Summer outside in a lathhouse
or bright dappled shade

Water and Humidity
Mist cork raft daily, more
often in hot weather
Set container on gravel in a
saucer filled with water
Water and mist container orchid once
a week, then twice a week after bloom
until pseudobulbs reach full size

Fertilizing Schedule
Every 2 weeks

Hardiness
Tender

When Blooms Appear
March to April

CATTLEYA SKINNERI, SAN SEBASTIAN ORCHID

I had long lusted after these delicate, rosy-colored, gracefully shaped orchids I studied in photographs and botanical illustrations. Imagine the shock when I arrived in El Salvador and found hundreds of them decorating the trees of parking lots around supermarkets. There they grow as natives, basking in the easy delight of a tropical climate. A small number of plants strapped on by landscapers spread and spread to every branch until the trees become loaded with handsomely generous plants and blossoms. ¶ San Sebastian orchids are bifoliates, meaning they have more than one leaf per pseudobulb and hence two or three times more flower stalks, which ensures they become covered with blossoms. The hybrid San Sebastians offer even more beautiful bloom than the species, and a range of pink to rose and lavender colors. ¶ **HOW TO DO IT** ¶ During the winter months, keep this cattleya on a south-, east- or west-facing windowsill, where it will receive sun in the morning or afternoon. The foliage should be light green, dark green indicating too little light. Place the pot on gravel in a saucer filled with water. In the summer the San Sebastian orchid benefits from placement outside in a lathhouse or brightly dappled shade, but be sure to maintain a high humidity by keeping the saucer filled with water. Water the plant once a week, twice a week during a summer heat spell. Feed it every two weeks with a 30-10-10 fertilizer diluted half-strength according to the directions on the container. Use medium-grade orchid bark as a potting mix, and repot after two years or when the mix has broken down to a fine texture.¶ As plants come into bloom, make sure to stake the blossoms. And while they flower, place them out of direct sunlight in a cool room but continue watering to extend the blossom period.

San Sebastian Orchid
Cattleya skinneri, *species or hybrid*

❧

What You Need
*30-10-10 orchid fertilizer,
diluted half-strength*

❧

When to Buy
In bloom

❧

Light
*Morning or afternoon sun
during winter months
Summer outside in a lathhouse or bright,
dappled shade*

❧

Water and Humidity
*Water weekly, more often in hot weather
Set container on gravel in a saucer filled
with water*

❧

Fertilizing Schedule
Every 2 weeks

❧

Hardiness
Tender

❧

When Blooms Appear
March to April

❧

Dendrobium phalaenopsis

Dendrobiums are tall for a windowsill, but irresistible because of their radiant blooms that last cheerily from autumn through the long dark months of winter. Sprays of them emerge from the tops of both the old and the new canes, each with ten or more flowers. ¶ Treat them as you would cattleyas: lots of bright light, and weekly watering. Mist the leaves during the hot days of summer. ¶ Dendrobiums like to be in small pots. Allow them to become cramped, and don't fuss about repotting them often because they prefer not to be disturbed. Repot only about every three years, using a medium-grade potting mix with an equal amount of lava rocks. When you set the plant into the potting mix, make sure not to plant too deeply, for the new growth spots, or "eyes," rot quickly if buried. ¶ You may discover your dendrobium forming plantlets, or keikis (Hawaiian for babies), at the nodes, complete with roots. When the keikis have grown leaves and root systems, cut them off and pot them up separately. ¶ **HOW TO DO IT** ¶ During the winter months, keep your dendrobium on a south-, east- or west-facing windowsill, where it will receive bright sun. The foliage should be light green, dark green indicating too little light. Place the pot on gravel in a saucer filled with water. In summer the plant can be placed outside in a lathhouse or bright, dappled shade, but be sure to maintain a high humidity by keeping the saucer filled with water and misting on hot days. Water the plant once a week, twice a week during a summer heat spell. Feed it every two weeks with a 30-10-10 fertilizer diluted half-strength according to directions on the container. Use medium-grade orchid bark with lava rocks as a potting mix, and repot every three years or when the potting mix has broken down to a fine texture. ¶ As plants come into bloom, make sure to stake the blossoms. And while they flower, place them out of direct sunlight in a cool room but continue watering to extend the blossom period.

Dendrobium phalaenopsis Hybrid

❧

What You Need
*30-10-10 orchid fertilizer,
diluted half-strength*

❧

When to Buy
In bloom

❧

Light
*Morning or afternoon sun
Summer outside in a lathhouse or bright,
dappled shade*

❧

Water and Humidity
*Water weekly, more often in hot weather
Set container on gravel in a saucer filled
with water; mist on hot summer days*

❧

Fertilizing Schedule
Every 2 weeks

❧

Hardiness
Tender

❧

When Blooms Appear
*September to March, depending
upon variety*

❧

Laeliocattleya

The intergeneric cross between laelia and cattleya orchids has created easily grown plants small enough for windowsills without sacrificing lovely blooms. These are the "you can have it all" orchids, easy to maintain, forgiving about occasional watering lapses, liking bright light, and blooming regularly and reliably. Even if the bloom is smaller than that of the big cattleya, it is still generous, glorious, and worth the wait. ¶ There are lots and lots of laeliocattleya hybrids available through orchid nurseries and specialty mail-ordering services. Because these plants are so reliable and so worthy, consider mail-ordering a number of different types to arrive as bare-root plants. Be ready to pot them up the instant they land on your doorstep in their cardboard box, all individually plastic-wrapped with their label taped to their leaves. Have available in advance a sack or more of medium-grade orchid bark mix, as well as the appropriate number of ceramic pots. ¶ Soak the potting mix for four hours before you plant the orchids. Secure each new plant in its container with a bamboo stake or a rhizome clip so it doesn't wiggle. As the roots grow, they secure the plant; the clip or stake steadies it until the roots are strong. Make sure to keep the labels in order as you pot each plant. Then sit back and wait with excited anticipation for a long series of blooms. It may take up to a year for the plants to flower, but you'll get a whole windowsill of orchid blooms for the price of a couple pots bought in a store. ¶ **HOW TO DO IT** ¶ During the winter months, keep your laeliocattleya on a south-, east-, or west-facing windowsill, where it will receive bright sun. The foliage should be light green, dark green indicating too little light. Place the pot on gravel in a saucer filled with water and mist daily. In the summer the plant benefits from placement outside in a lathhouse or bright, dappled shade, but be sure to maintain a high humidity by misting and keeping the saucer filled with water. Water the plant once a week, twice a week during a summer heat spell. Feed it every ✦

Laeliocattleya Hybrid

What You Need
30-10-10 orchid fertilizer, diluted half-strength

When to Buy
In bloom

Light
Morning or afternoon sun during winter months
Summer outside in a lathhouse or bright, dappled shade

Water and Humidity
Water weekly, more often in hot weather
Set container on gravel in a saucer filled with water
Mist daily in the early morning

Fertilizing Schedule
Every 2 weeks

Hardiness
Tender

When Blooms Appear
Spring and summer, depending upon variety

two weeks with a 30-10-10 fertilizer diluted half-strength according to the directions on the container. Use medium-grade orchid bark as a potting mix, and repot after two years if the mix has broken down to a fine texture. ¶ As plants come into bloom, make sure to stake the blossoms. And while they flower, place them out of direct sunlight in a cool room but continue watering to extend bloom.

LUDISIA DISCOLOR, JEWEL ORCHID

Unlike the many orchids that sit for long periods of time as an inconspicuous set of leaves bereft of interest until the sudden burst of bloom, jewel orchid is beloved foremost for its fabulous, year-round multicolored leaves. In point of fact, these orchids are often sold without a mention of their charming—if miniature—blooms. ¶ The foliage is reddish green and seemingly patterned by an artist's fine pencil with thin parallel lines shadowed in red with white echoes. It's handsomely shown off on the creeping stems that will grow upright or cascade over the sides of a hanging container. Try to find the largest plants you can, for it may take some time for an immature plant to produce the white half-inch flowers dotted with yellow lips that cover the straight flower stalks. An ideal houseplant because it doesn't like bright light, the jewel orchid lives happily in a warm room if kept moist and regularly fertilized. ¶ **HOW TO DO IT** ¶ All year, keep your jewel orchid on a north-facing windowsill, where your hand does not cast a shadow. Place the pot on gravel in a saucer filled with water. Water the plant once a week, twice a week during a summer heat spell. Feed it every two weeks with a 30-10-10 fertilizer, diluted half-strength according to directions on the container. Use a container potting mix, and only repot when the plant seems to stop thriving.

Jewel Orchid
Ludisia discolor, *also known as*
Haemaria discolor
❧

What You Need
*30-10-10 orchid fertilizer,
diluted half-strength*
❧

When to Buy
When large plants are available
❧

Light
*Light shade; your hand should
not cast a shadow*
❧

Water and Humidity
*Water weekly, more often in hot weather
Set container on gravel in a saucer
filled with water*
❧

Fertilizing Schedule
Every 2 weeks
❧

Hardiness
Tender
❧

When Blooms Appear
February to March
❧

ONCIDIUM, DANCING DOLLS

Hybrid oncidiums bear sprays of individual flowers that seem to dance in the air, dolls dressed in fanciful costumes. Some grow quite large, squeezing only onto the benches of a spacious greenhouse, so make sure to take home a hybrid of small to medium size. Many have the characteristic yellow and orangish colors that have given them the nickname in Central America of huevos con chorizo, eggs and sausage. Others are pink or lavender. Although the flowers are small, the combined effect of the many blossoms on each stem is of a whole troupe of dancers filling the stage at once. ¶ Like cattleyas, these orchids like their light bright. Give them lots and lots of light. In the summer, make sure to place them outside in a lathhouse. ¶ **HOW TO DO IT** ¶ During the winter months, keep your dancing doll on a south-, east-, or west-facing windowsill, where it will receive bright sun. The foliage should be light green, dark green indicating too little light. Place the pot on gravel in a saucer filled with water. In the summer the plant benefits from placement outside in a lathhouse or bright, dappled shade, but be sure to maintain high humidity by keeping the saucer filled with water. Water the plant once a week, twice a week during a summer heat spell. Feed it every two weeks with a 30-10-10 fertilizer diluted half-strength according to the directions on the container. Use medium-grade orchid bark as a potting mix, and repot after two years if the mix has broken down to a fine texture. ¶ As plants come into bloom, make sure to stake the blossoms. And while they flower, place them out of direct sunlight in a cool room but continue watering to extend the blossom period.

Dancing Dolls Hybrids
Oncidium 'Moonlight Chandelier,' 'Golden Peacock,' or Killer Bees

What You Need
30-10-10 fertilizer, diluted half-strength

When to Buy
In bloom

Light
Morning or afternoon sun during winter months
Summer outside in a lathhouse or bright, dappled shade

Water and Humidity
Water weekly, more often in hot weather
Set container on gravel in a saucer filled with water

Fertilizing Schedule
Every 2 weeks

Hardiness
Tender

When Blooms Appear
December to April

ONCIDIUM FLEXUOSUM

Not all orchids show off with humungous blooms in poster paint colors. Many orchids bloom modestly with flowers in miniature. This gem-like quality lends the little blooms particular charm, making them as desirable as their fantastic and fashionable giant relatives. This small plant may be difficult to locate, but orchid fanciers, botanical gardens, and specialty nurseries will be able to find some stock for you because its cheery canary yellow flowers with orange splashes and easy growth habit make it a favorite. It also spreads rapidly, which means you may soon find yourself with extra plants to share or trade back. ¶ *Oncidium flexuosum* runs up a tree trunk in its native habitat, so this is a variety that grows best mounted on a cork bark raft. If you prefer, you can grow it in a ceramic pot with medium-grade potting mix, letting the roots hang out the bottom of the pot and misting them daily. ¶ Water and feed the little plants as you would cattleyas, letting them dry out between waterings if you are growing them in pots but misting plants growing on rafts daily. ¶ **HOW TO DO IT** ¶ During the winter months, keep your oncidium on a south-, east-, or west-facing windowsill, where it will receive bright sun. The foliage should be light green, dark green indicating too little light. Mist the cork bark raft every day, and more often during hot, dry summer days. If you're growing this orchid in a pot, place it on gravel in a saucer filled with water. If the plant is on a cork raft, mist exposed roots daily. In the summer the plant benefits from placement outside in a lathhouse or bright, dappled shade, but be sure to maintain a high humidity by misting the roots and, if potted, keeping the pot saucer filled with water. Water a potted plant once a week, twice a week during a summer heat

Oncidium flexuosum

❧

What You Need
*30-10-10 orchid fertilizer,
diluted half-strength*

❧

When to Buy
In bloom

❧

Light
*Morning or afternoon sun during
winter months
Summer outside in a lathhouse or bright,
dappled shade*

❧

Water and Humidity
*Mist cork raft every day,
Water pot once a week, twice a week during
a heat spell; mist exposed roots daily
Set container on gravel in a saucer
filled with water*

❧

Fertilizing Schedule
Every 2 weeks

❧

Hardiness
Tender

❧

When Blooms Appear
March to April

❧

spell. Feed it every two weeks with a 30-10-10 fertilizer diluted half-strength according to the directions on the container. Use a cork bark raft with a bedding of sphagnum moss, or fill a pot with fine-grade orchid bark mix and repot after two years if the mix has broken down to a fine texture. While they flower, place them out of direct sunlight in a cool room but continue watering to extend the blossom period.

Paphiopedilum, lady's slipper orchid

The shape of their long-lasting flowers has given these orchids the common name of lady's slipper orchids. With their diversity of colors, Cinderella could have had a rainbow selection to choose from instead of wearing a plain old glass slipper. Because lady's slipper orchids are so easily hybridized, there are countless varieties in different sizes, colors, and shapes. They make great houseplants because the low light levels of our homes duplicate their native forest floor environment. ¶ The foliage of the maudiae varieties is heavily mottled, making them interesting as houseplants even when they are out of bloom. Growers used to follow different regimens for mottled- and plain-leaf varieties, but no longer. House temperatures suit both types just fine. ¶ Terrestrial orchids without pseudobulbs, lady's slipper orchids need constant moisture, so grow them in plastic or glazed ceramic pots to help conserve moisture in the potting mix. Because they normally live in the leaf litter of forest floors, use a fine-grade orchid bark or a cymbidium mix when you repot them. ¶ **HOW TO DO IT** ¶ During the winter months, keep your lady's slipper orchid on a windowsill, where your hand does not cast a shadow. Place the pot on gravel in a saucer filled with water. Mist the plant daily. In the summer the plant benefits from placement outside in a lathhouse or shady spot, but be sure to maintain a high humidity by misting and keeping the saucer filled with water. Water the plant twice a week, more during a summer heat spell. Feed it every two weeks with a 30-10-10 fertilizer diluted half-strength according to the directions on the container. Use fine-grade orchid bark or a cymbidium mix as a potting soil, repotting after two years if the mix has broken down to a finer texture. ¶ As plants come into bloom, make sure to stake each blossom. And while they flower, place them out of direct sunlight in a cool room but continue watering to extend the blossom period.

Lady's Slipper Orchid
Paphiopedilum hybrid, mottled leaf or plain leaf

❧

What You Need
30-10-10 orchid fertilizer, diluted half-strength

❧

When to Buy
In bloom

❧

Light
Light shade; your hand should not cast a shadow
Summer outside in a lathhouse or shady spot

❧

Water and Humidity
Water twice weekly, more often in hot weather
Set container on gravel in a saucer filled with water
Mist daily

❧

Fertilizing Schedule
Every 2 weeks

❧

Hardiness
To 40°F for plain-leaf types, 55°F for mottled-leaf types

❧

When Blooms Appear
Fall to winter for plain-leaf types; summer or winter for mottled-leaf types

❧

PHALAENOPSIS AMABILIS HYBRIDS, MOTH ORCHID

These widely available orchids ensnare orchid fanciers with the graceful arch of their flowering stem, so afloat with blossoms that they earn their name "moth orchids." They merit attention because of the beauty of their blossom, the long-lastingness of their bloom—as long as three months—and their inclination to rebloom the same year, all with minimal fuss. ¶ Their native habitats are the warm, moist jungles of Asia, New Guinea, and the Philippines, and the tropical areas of Australia. Epiphytes, their home provides them with warmth, humidity, and rain to keep their exposed roots moist. Yet, housed in plastic containers with orchid bark and gravel trays to provide humidity, they adapt well to house temperatures of about 68°F. ¶ Moth orchids do not want dry roots, so make sure to water them consistently, before the potting mix totally dries out. Water your plants in the morning, because it is easy to catch water in the crown of the plant's leaves that will evaporate during the day, but if left overnight will contribute to crown rot. Mist your plants daily. ¶ After a long period of bloom, the flowers gradually fall off. Cut the blossom stem back to the last bloom point. A new branch may appear on the same stalk, bringing another season of bloom. ¶ Now available are phalaenopsis minis—plants that grow to the same size as the regular moth orchids but with many, many charming blossoms half the size of the regular varieties. All the moth orchids produce more flowers on each stem as the plants mature. ¶ **HOW TO DO IT** ¶ During the winter months, keep your moth orchid on a north-facing windowsill, where your hand does not cast a shadow. Place the pot on gravel in a saucer filled with water and mist daily in the early morning. In the summer the plant benefits from placement outside in a shady spot, but be sure to maintain a high humidity by keeping the saucer filled with water and misting daily in the morning. Water the plant twice a week, more often if necessary during a summer heat spell. Feed it every two weeks with a 30-10-10 fertilizer diluted half-

Moth Orchid

Phalaenopsis amabilis *hybrid*

❧

What You Need
30-10-10 orchid fertilizer,
diluted half-strength

❧

When to Buy
In bloom

❧

Light
*Light shade; your hand should
not cast a shadow*
*Summer outside in a lathhouse
or shady spot*

❧

Water and Humidity
*Water twice weekly in the morning,
more often in hot weather*
*Set container on gravel in a saucer
filled with water*
Mist daily, in the early morning

❧

Fertilizing Schedule
Every 2 weeks

❧

Hardiness
To 60°F

❧

When Blooms Appear
*November to May, with possible rebloom
3 months later*

❧

strength according to the directions on the container. Use medium-grade orchid bark as a potting mix, and repot after one year if roots are visible through the holes in the bottom of the pot; otherwise, wait two years. Moth orchids do not like overcrowding. Look for the bright green root tips that develop after blooming and signal the right time to repot. ¶ As plants come into bloom, make sure to stake each stem. After buds fatten, do not change the plant's position or the blooms may become twisted. And while they flower, place them out of direct sunlight in a cool room but continue watering to extend the blossom period. When all the blossoms on the flower spike have faded, cut it back to just below the lowest blossom. The orchid may develop a new side spike and rebloom in about three months.

ORCHIDS TO
GROW IN
OUTDOOR
CONTAINERS

Orchids from high-elevation habitats prefer living outside most of the year, languishing when cooped up and housebound. These orchids want more than a summer outside; they really want the breezes, the sunlight, and the year-round fluctuation in temperatures. ❧ For mild-winter gardeners, the toughest task becomes finding the location with the right amount of light, and out of the grueling noon sun. Underneath trees or porch overhangs, where slanting rays of early morning or afternoon sun reach the orchids, can provide the perfect growing spot. Gardeners with snow-filled winters need to find the right summer spot and also a winter place for their orchids that protects them from freezing temperatures while providing lots of bright sunshine. South-facing closed porches, unheated westerly rooms, or windowed garages attached to the house can all provide the safety from frost and the light your orchids need. ❧ Knowing these orchids prefer the out-of-doors may lead the gardener to assume they can survive the rough-and-ready life of camping out with little attention. Unlike the snugly cosseted indoor types, which are also under your eye daily as you pass them by, you may not check your outdoor plants as rigorously, and they'll likely suffer. ❧ Slugs and snails can hide close by, coming out at night to feast on the flower buds and new growth, as much a gourmet delicacy to them as caviar is to us. Mice and rats may picnic on the pseudobulbs. Early rains leave stagnant water in the tender cavities, rotting out new growth or plant crowns. ❧ Even though these orchids are hardier in terms of temperature, make sure to water and feed them regularly, mist them when temperatures climb, and check the foliage for any pest damage. Plants that form blooms during rainy seasons should be protected under a porch overhang, but be sure to water them regularly. If you live in an area with snowy winters, protect orchids when the temperature begins to drop by moving them indoors.

CYMBIDIUM

Arching sprays with double rows of blooms in colors from green through gold, pink, or even tawny to rusty brown—cymbidiums in bloom take one's breath away. It's almost a secret that these plants are just about as easy to take care of and have bloom for you as geraniums, as long as you provide the climate they need and feed and water them generously. ¶ Keep the light bright for cymbidiums. They prefer morning and afternoon dappled sun, a level of brightness that keeps their leaves a light yellowy green. Leave them out in the fall for chilling (although never below 40°F) to encourage them to set the gorgeous spikes for which they are so famous. Large plants will throw four to six bloom spikes every year. ¶ Gardeners who live in cold-winter climates bring cymbidiums indoors in late autumn to a cool, sunny porch when temperatures begin to regularly fall below 45°F. Although they are hardy enough to stand lower temperatures for a short period of time, the bloom spikes are tender and can be injured. If you live in a mild-winter climate, the plants can stay outdoors all year long, but protect the bloom spikes from rains, which can damage the blossoms. A sheltering roof overhang protects the blossoms without restricting light. Cymbidiums stay in bloom for months; you can bring them indoors, but display them in a coolish room for longest bloom. ¶ When plants fill their containers, repot. You can transfer the whole plant to a larger container, or if the plant has six or more pseudobulbs carrying leaves, you can divide it. Make sure each division has at least three live bulbs—bulbs with leaves. Bulbs without leaves, called back bulbs, usually will sprout, but not produce flowers for three or four years. ¶ **HOW TO DO IT** ¶ In cold climates, leave your cymbidium outside as long as possible in the fall until frost threatens. Overwinter it inside in a brightly lit location where the temperature does not regularly drop below 45°F, placing it outside again in the spring only after all chance of frost has passed. In milder climates, place your

Cymbidium Hybrid

What You Need
30-10-10 orchid fertilizer,
diluted half-strength
0-10-10 orchid fertilizer,
diluted half-strength

When to Buy
In bloom

Light
Morning and afternoon dappled sun

Water and Humidity
Water weekly, more often in hot weather,
less often in winter

Fertilizing Schedule
30-10-10 fertilizer every 2 weeks
from January to July
0-10-10 fertilizer every 2 weeks
from August to December

Hardiness
To 30°F, but protect from frost

When Blooms Appear
November to May, depending on variety

cymbidium outside where it receives morning and afternoon dappled sun. The leaves should always be light green. Dark green leaves indicate too little light. Feed the plant a 30-10-10 fertilizer diluted half-strength according to the directions every two weeks from January to July. Switch to a low-nitrogen, 0-10-10, fertilizer diluted half-strength according to the directions from August to December. Water consistently, at least once a week, more often if weather becomes hot, less often in winter. Never let it dry out, but do not overwater and cause the roots to rot. ¶ As plants come into bloom, make sure to stake the blossoms. If you bring them inside while they flower, place them out of direct sunlight in a cool room but continue watering to extend the blossom period. Cut off bloom stalks after they fade, and gently pull off dead leaves. ¶ Repot immedi-ately after flowering into a larger container if the plant totally fills its existing container or repot in the same container with fresh potting mix if the orchid bark has broken down to a fine texture. Use a cymbidium mix or one-half coarse-grade orchid bark and one-half container potting mix. Cut off any dead or rotted roots. Center the plant in the container and fill with potting mix to within 1 inch of the rim. Gently press mix down around the outside of the container, making sure the pseudobulbs or back bulbs are only partially buried, with just the bottom third of each bulb beneath the mix. Stake or use a rhizome clip to steady the plant. Water thoroughly, then stop watering for two weeks, just misting and spraying the leaves to stimulate root growth.

Dendrobium kingianum

This Australian species orchid has been hybridized to produce miniature stems covered with white or pink blossoms, some with plain and some with speckled lips, and all very fragrant. Kingianums never grow much larger than 2 feet tall, but in spring they become covered with blooms that last up to a month. ¶ What is particularly beguiling about kingianums is their preference for outdoor living; indeed, in mild-winter climates they can be left outside all year long. Just like cymbidiums, they like morning and afternoon dappled sun. The trickiest part of caring for these easy orchids is protecting their winter-forming flower stalks from rainstorms, which can damage the developing buds. If you live in a snowy climate, overwinter your orchids on a bright, cool porch with temperatures that remain above 40°F. ¶ **HOW TO DO IT** ¶ In cold climates, overwinter your kingianum in a brightly lit location where the temperature does not drop below 40°F, placing it outside only after all chance of frost has passed. In milder climates, place the plant outside where it receives morning and afternoon dappled sun. The leaves should always be light green. Dark green leaves indicate too little light. Feed the plant a high-nitrogen, 30-10-10, fertilizer diluted full-strength every two weeks from January to August. Switch to a low-nitrogen, 0-10-10, fertilizer diluted half-strength from September to December, continuing to feed every two weeks. Water consistently, at least once a week, more often if weather becomes hot. Never let the plant dry out, but do not overwater and cause the roots to rot. Cut off bloom stalks after they fade, and gently pull off dead leaves. Repot immediately after flowering into a larger container if the plant totally fills its existing container, or repot in the same container with fine-grade orchid mix if the orchid bark has broken down to a fine texture.

Dendrobium kingianum

What You Need
30-10-10 orchid fertilizer,
diluted full-strength
0-10-10 orchid fertilizer,
diluted half-strength

When to Buy
In bloom

Light
Morning and afternoon dappled sun

Water and Humidity
Water weekly, more often hot weather

Fertilizing Schedule
30-10-10 every 2 weeks from
January to July
0-10-10 every 2 weeks from
August to December

Hardiness
To 40°F

When Blooms Appear
January to April, depending on variety

EPIDENDRUM IBAGUENSE

Whizzing along highways in Mexico, you may see tall plants growing next to the highway crowned with rosettes of small red, orange, or yellow flowers. Indeed, dotting the countryside, they don't seem worth a second look. Closer examination brings an exclamation of surprise, for these are orchids. ¶ Epidendrums' easy habits and simple cultivation make them great container plants, living outside casually during the summer, overwintering outside or in, depending on night temperatures. They like a sunny exposure, but as they don't have pseudobulbs, they should not dry out between waterings. If you live in a mild-winter climate, you also have the option of growing these orchids as terrestrials. In freezing weather, they should be sheltered like your cymbidiums. Epidendrums may repeat bloom for you throughout the year, and they are dramatic as cut flowers. ¶ **HOW TO DO IT** ¶ In cold climates, leave your epidendrum outside as long as possible in the fall until frost threatens. Overwinter it inside in a brightly lit location where the temperature does not drop below 50°F, placing it outside again in the spring only after all chance of frost has passed. In milder climates, place the plant outside where it receives morning and afternoon sun. The leaves should always be light green. Dark green leaves indicate too little light. Feed the plant a 30-10-10 fertilizer diluted half-strength according to the directions on the container every two weeks. Water consistently, at least once a week, more often if weather becomes hot, less often in winter. Never let it dry out, but do not overwater and cause the roots to rot. ¶ Cut off bloom stalks after they fade. Repot immediately after flowering into a larger container if the plant totally ✦

fills its existing container, or repot in the same container with fresh potting mix if the orchid bark has broken down to a fine texture. Use a cymbidium mix, or one-half medium-grade orchid bark and one-half container potting mix. Cut off any dead or rotted roots. Center the plant in the container and fill with potting mix. Gently press mix down around the outside of the container and fill to within 1 inch of the rim. Stake or use a rhizome clip to steady the plant. Water thoroughly, then stop watering for two weeks, just misting and spraying the leaves to stimulate root growth.

Miniature Cymbidium

Miniature cymbidium hybrids promise the same number of exquisite arching bloom spikes as the standard cyms—albeit the flowers are smaller—the same range of exquisite colors, and the extended length of bloom, all on a more compact, easy-to-manage plant not out of scale in smaller gardens. Easier to repot, easier to move indoors to display the bloom, and just as easy to grow, these orchids promise a lot, and they deliver. ¶ Mini-cyms are just a bit tricky to buy, because some grow up to be almost as big as the so-called standard cymbidium, not miniature one bit! When purchasing your plant, make sure to inquire how large the mature orchid grows. ¶ In contrast to standard cymbidiums, minis set bloom easily. They don't need the low temperatures to trigger bloom spikes. As autumn comes, with cooler temperatures at night, leave the plant outside until freezing temperatures are predicted. Although the plant can take a light frost, the tender bloom stalks will be damaged by too much icy exposure. ¶ **HOW TO DO IT** ¶ In cold climates, leave your miniature cymbidium outside as long as possible in the fall until frost threatens. Overwinter it inside in a brightly lit location where the temperature does not regularly drop below 45°F, placing it outside again in the spring only after all chance of frost has passed. In milder climates, place your cymbidium outside where it receives morning and afternoon dappled sun. The leaves should always be light green. Dark green leaves indicate too little light. Feed the plant a 30-10-10 fertilizer diluted half-strength every two weeks according to directions on the container from January to July. Switch to a low-nitrogen, 0-10-10, fertilizer diluted half-strength according to directions on the container from August to December. Water consistently, at least once a week, more often if weather becomes hot, less often in winter. Never let it dry out, but do not over-water and cause the roots to rot. ¶ As plants come into bloom, make sure to stake the blossoms. If you bring them inside while they flower, place them out of direct sun- ✒

Miniature Cymbidium Hybrid
❧

What You Need
30-10-10 orchid fertilizer,
diluted half-strength
0-10-10 orchid fertilizer,
diluted half-strength
❧

When to Buy
In bloom
❧

Light
Morning and afternoon dappled sun
❧

Water and Humidity
Water weekly, more often in hot weather,
less often in winter
❧

Fertilizing Schedule
30-10-10 fertilizer every 2 weeks
from January to July
0-10-10 fertilizer every 2 weeks
from August to December
❧

Hardiness
To 30°F, but protect from frost
❧

When Blooms Appear
November to May, depending on variety
❧

light in a cool room but continue watering to extend the blossom period. Cut off bloom stalks after they fade, and gently pull off dead leaves. ¶ Repot immediately after flowering into a larger container if the plant totally fills its existing container or repot in the same container with fresh potting mix if the orchid bark has broken down to a fine texture. Use a cymbidium mix or one-half coarse-grade orchid bark and one-half container potting mix. Cut off any dead or rotted roots. Center the plant in the container and fill with potting mix to within 1 inch of the rim. Make sure the pseudobulbs and back bulbs are only partially buried, with just the bottom third of each bulb beneath the mix. Stake or use a rhizome clip to steady the plant. Water thoroughly, then stop watering for two weeks, just misting and spraying the leaves to stimulate root growth.

Zygopetalum mackayi

Once you are familiar with cymbidium culture, you can easily add a zygopetalum to your collection or, of course, vice versa. The tall bloom stalks bear two-toned flowers: green spotted petals and a wonderfully garish, extravagantly sized purple-and-white striped lip. They exude a fragrance reminiscent of hyacinths, which, it must be admitted, some find cloying in a shuttered room. ¶ Like cymbidiums, these orchids need high-nitrogen fertilizer during their growth period, in spring and summer, and then exist happily with low-nitrogen fertilizer. Their leaves will grow up to 2 feet long, and they may outgrow their container faster than most of your more slowpoke orchid varieties. Let them follow along with your cymbidium care, and you will be rewarded with generous, exotic blooms during the gray, dingy winter months. ¶ **HOW TO DO IT** ¶ In cold climates, leave your zygopetalum outside as long as possible in the fall until frost threatens. Overwinter it inside in a brightly lit location where the temperature does not drop below 45°F, placing it outside again in the spring only after all chance of frost has passed. In milder climates, place your zygopetalum outside where it receives dappled sun. The leaves should always be light green. Dark green leaves indicate too little light. Feed the plant a 30-10-10 fertilizer diluted full-strength every two weeks. Water consistently, at least once a week, more often if weather becomes hot, less often in winter. Never let it dry out, but do not overwater and cause the roots to rot. ¶ As plants come into bloom, make sure to stake the blossoms. If you bring them inside while they flower, place them out of direct sunlight in a cool room but continue watering to extend the blossom period. Cut off bloom stalks after they fade, and gently pull off dead leaves. ¶ Repot immediately after flowering into a larger container if the plant totally fills its existing container, or repot in the ✒

Zygopetalum mackayi, Z. intermedium

❧

What You Need
30-10-10 orchid fertilizer, diluted full-strength
0-10-10 orchid fertilizer, diluted half-strength

❧

When to Buy
In bloom

❧

Light
Morning and afternoon sun

❧

Water and Humidity
Water weekly, more often in hot weather, less often in winter

❧

Fertilizing Schedule
30-10-10 fertilizer every 2 weeks from January to July
0-10-10 fertilizer every 2 weeks from August to December

❧

Hardiness
To 30°F, but protect from frost

❧

When Blooms Appear
November to May, depending on variety

❧

same container with fresh potting mix if the orchid bark has broken down to a fine texture. Use coarse-grade orchid potting mix. Cut off any dead or rotted roots. Center the plant in the container and fill with potting mix. Gently press mix down around the outside of the container and continue to fill to within 1 inch of the rim. Make sure the pseudobulbs sit on top of the mix, not buried. Use a rhizome clip to steady the plant. Water thoroughly.

ORCHIDS
TO GROW
IN THE
GROUND

When we think of orchids living in the wild, we generally imagine tropical orchids growing on trees, their glorious blooms shining in the dappled sunshine

and their roots hanging down like hair. In our mind's eye, the only other orchids live in greenhouses, rows upon rows of them lining benches in rainbow colors of blooms. ❧ Yet because orchids come from so many different parts of the world, it only makes sense that loads of orchids grow successfully with their feet planted squarely in the ground. Some of these terrestrial types even survive with a blanket of snow over them in winter; the others require mild-winter climates. A major setback to cultivating a wide variety of terrestrial orchids is their need for a specific soil organism that converts organic material to nutrients the orchid roots can absorb. For this reason, many, if not most, terrestrial orchids do not survive transplanting. ❧ There are, however, a few types that can be grown at home successfully, and these make good garden companions. Although some terrestrial species orchids live in swamps and bogs, the orchids in this book have water-sensitive roots that rot in soggy conditions, so make sure to work in plenty of compost and organic matter to allow the soil to drain quickly. After you have the soil thoroughly combined with the compost, dig a small hole 6 inches deep, fill it with water, and time how long it takes for the water to completely drain out. It must empty within five minutes, without fail. ❧ When buying terrestrial orchids, make sure to deal with nurseries that raise and sell only their own propagated stock. Illegal gathering of terrestrial orchids threatens many native populations, and since transplanting seldom succeeds, a precious resource is wasted.

BLETILLA STRIATA, CHINESE GROUND ORCHID

These little, bright orchids with miniature 1- to 2-inch blooms grow easily in your garden. Widely available both in catalogues and nurseries, they look like ordinary bulb corms. Find them for sale in early spring mixed among the summer-flowering bulb displays. Once planted, these orchids quickly send up bright green, crinkled leaves, which can grow from 18 inches to 24 inches tall. Soon after the white or lavender-pinky blooms appear, particularly entrancing in their miniatureness. There are some types with variegated leaves. ¶ Use Chinese ground orchids clumped together, but near the front of your garden beds or in containers so you won't miss the display of their blooms. If your winter temperatures drop to and stay below 20°F, consider mulching your plants in fall with a thick covering of hay, or planting them under an overhang to protect them from the cold. Like ordinary garden bulbs, the foliage dies back in fall and the corm stays dormant through the winter. ¶ The only tricky part of growing Chinese ground orchids is remembering to withhold water in the spring so the blooms can develop before the rush of foliage. Once you see bloom stalks or leaves about 4 inches high, start to water again cautiously. ¶ **HOW TO DO IT** ¶ Choose plump, healthy corms that show no signs of shriveling or injury. Prepare the garden soil by digging in organic compost to lighten it. Add a pelleted, slow-release low-nitrogen fertilizer to the soil. Water the soil thoroughly. Plant the corms 2 inches deep and 4 inches apart. Do not water until the shoots are 4 to 6 inches high or until you can see the stems of the flowers. After the plants have bloomed, apply a yearly application of pelleted slow-release, low-nitrogen fertilizer according to the directions. Do not cut off the leaves as they die down in the fall. Mulch thickly with hay if winter temperatures tend to drop lower than 20°F.

Chinese Ground Orchid
Bletilla striata (pink) or
B. striata 'Alba' (white)
❧

What You Need
6 corms
1 square foot of prepared ground
Organic compost
Pelleted, slow-release low-nitrogen fertilizer
❧

When to Buy
Early spring, from mail-order catalogues
and nurseries
❧

When to Plant
As soon as the ground can be
worked in spring
❧

Light
Light shade
❧

Water and Humidity
Light watering throughout summer
❧

Fertilizing Schedule
When planting and after bloom
❧

Hardiness
To 20°F
❧

When Blooms Appear
May to June
❧

Pleione formosana

Who wouldn't be proud to take guests around the garden and point out small orchids abloom? These little pleiones add to anyone's spring garden, and although they have some important cultural rules, once established, they should grow easily for you. Pleiones come from Asia, some living in dappled shade along the edges of forests and other varieties growing up the mountain slopes in Tibet. Although they are extremely tolerant of cold—they grow outside in the coldest winter areas—they do need some tender care to transplant successfully to your garden. ¶ Make sure to do lots of soil preparation before you set in the bulbs early in spring. When planting, don't bury the bulbs; plant them above the soil. Once they are set out, do not water until the leaves begin to grow. ¶ Once the plants have bloomed, be sure to keep the soil moist all summer and fall. Pleiones do not like their roots to dry out. ¶ **HOW TO DO IT** ¶ Choose plump, healthy corms that show no signs of shriveling or injury. Prepare the garden soil by digging in organic compost to lighten it. Add a pelleted, slow-release low-nitrogen fertilizer to the soil. Water the soil thoroughly. Plant the corms 2 inches deep and 2 inches apart. Do not water until the shoots are 4 to 6 inches high or until you can see the stems of the flowers. After the plants have bloomed, apply a yearly application of pelleted slow-release, low-nitrogen fertilizer according to the directions. Do not cut off the leaves as they die down in the fall. Mulch thickly with hay if winter temperatures tend to drop lower than 20°F.

**Pleione formosana,
P. bulbocodioides**

❧

What You Need
6 corms
1 square foot of prepared ground
Organic compost
Pelleted slow-release, low-nitrogen fertilizer

❧

When to Buy
Early spring, from mail-order
catalogues and nurseries

❧

When to Plant
As soon as the ground can be
worked in spring

❧

Light
Light shade

❧

Water and Humidity
Light watering throughout summer

❧

Fertilizing Schedule
When planting and after bloom

❧

Hardiness
To 20°F

❧

When Blooms Appear
May to June

❧

EXOTIC

ORCHIDS

Beginning orchid growers find themselves seduced by the gorgeous beauty of phalaenopsis or the strange and wonderful paphiopedilum, plants with showy blossoms

and ease of care. Although the passion for these beauties may not fade, the challenge of going up to the next level, trying something just a bit more unusual, can sneak up on an orchid grower. Suddenly, the reliable bloom of an old favorite seems just a little too predictable, and the rarer blooms of species orchids or the less common hybrids that need to be raised from baby-sizes seem a rewarding adventure. ❧ Exotic orchids are not guaranteed to be simple; they claim some ticklish coaxing. You may need to search them out, for rarely do they reside in nurseries or florists shops. Look for them in specialty orchid nurseries, botanical gardens, or mail-order catalogues. ❧ Do your homework first. Compare your home environment with the needs of these orchids. Be prepared to fret over them a bit more than your old reliables. Realize that raising these plants may call for you to explore some of the more advanced, technical aspects of orchid growing, perhaps using indoor lights timed to seasonal requirements or setting up specialized fertilizing routines. But like any orchid, exotic orchids flourish easily when their needs are met, so your challenge is simply in modifying your environment to charm them into bloom.

CATTLEYA

Who doesn't remember the rapture of either giving or receiving their first prom orchid? Nestled in a box with a cellophane window that rattled slightly, the cattleya bloom with its appropriately colored bow and pearl-tipped pin glowed with the promise of the evening's excitement. ¶ Despite their exotic dress, cattleyas are actually one of the easiest varieties of orchids to grow, except for one factor: They simply must have light—lots and lots and lots of strong light. A light green leaf tells you the plant is receiving enough light. Rich dark green leaves indicate not enough light. ¶ Some of the full-size cattleyas are giants, a mature plant growing up to 2 feet tall, making them almost too tall for a windowsill. Still, they are so uncomplaining of their care and so rewarding in their bloom and fragrance that making room for them seems the least you can do. ¶ In their native habitat of the South American tropics, cattleyas attach themselves to tree crotches or rocks, with their roots exposed to the air. Consequently, to grow them at home, provide them with a medium-grade mix and water them so that they dry out between waterings, as they do in their native habitat. Cattleyas must be protected indoors during the cold winter months, but they prefer outside living during the summer. Be sure to shade them from noontime sun by placing them in a lathhouse or underneath trees, and mist them if temperatures climb over 80°F. If your plant does not rebloom for you, purchase a growing lamp and focus it on the cattleya for five hours a day during the winter months to boost the light level. ¶ **HOW TO DO IT** ¶ During the winter months, provide as much bright sunny light as you can for your cattleya by placing it on a south-, east-, or west-facing windowsill, where it will receive bright sun. The foliage should be light green, dark green indicating too little light. Place the pot on gravel in a saucer filled with water. In summer the plant can be placed outside in a lathhouse or a bright, sun-dappled spot, but be sure to maintain a high humidity by misting during heat spells ✤

Cattleya Hybrid

What You Need
*30-10-10 orchid fertilizer,
diluted half-strength*

When to Buy
In bloom

Light
*Morning and afternoon sun
Summer outside in a lathhouse or in bright,
dappled sunshine*

Water and Humidity
*Water weekly, more often during
summer heat spells
Set container over gravel in a saucer
filled with water
Mist when temperatures exceed 80°F*

Fertilizing Schedule
*30-10-10 every 2 weeks
from March to October
30-10-10 once a month
from November through February*

Hardiness
Tender

When Blooms Appear
November to March

and keeping the saucer filled with water. Water the plant once a week, twice a week if necessary during a summer heat spell. Feed it with a 30-10-10 fertilizer diluted half-strength every two weeks during the growing season, from March to October, then once a month from November through February. Use medium-grade orchid bark as a potting mix, and repot after two years if the mix has broken down to a fine texture. ¶ As plants come into bloom, make sure to stake the blossoms. And while they flower, place them out of direct sunlight in a cool room but continue watering to extend the blossom period.

Dendrobium nobile

Dendrobium nobile looks so glamorous you might suppose that only experts could produce such a specimen. The flowers cover the tall stems in colors from white to dainty pink and deep magenta purples. Nobiles want special attention paid to their watering and fertilizing schedules, and you must locate places indoors or out where these light lovers can receive lots of bright light. However, with a bit of TLC, your plants will produce literally hundreds of flowers for you. ¶ Nobiles can become light-starved with ordinary house living, so successful growers find them outside locations where they can luxuriate in bright, dappled sunlight all summer without direct sun burning the leaves. Because nobiles come from mountain regions, they need cool autumn temperatures, as do cymbidiums, to trigger their blossom production, so don't hurry them inside until night temperatures drop to 40°F. In cold-winter areas, overwinter your nobile inside in a brightly lit location where the temperature does not drop below 50°F, placing it outside again in the spring only after all chance of frost has passed. ¶ The fertilizing and watering schedule changes by season. Nobiles need to go almost dormant in winter or they won't flower. As with other dendrobiums, keep the nobile pot small when repotting. Use a 3-inch pot for a plant 5 inches tall, a 4-inch pot for a 12-inch plant. Should the plant develop keikis, let the roots develop to 3 inches long, then cut away the plantlets and pot them in 3-inch containers. ¶ **HOW TO DO IT** ¶ During the winter months, keep the dendrobium on a south-, east-, or west-facing windowsill, where it will receive bright sun. The foliage should be light green, dark green indicating too little light. In the summer the plant benefits from placement outside in a lathhouse or a bright, sun-dappled spot. In spring, as the temperature rises above 50°F, begin to water and fertilize every two weeks. Feed your nobile with a 30-10-10 fertilizer diluted half-strength according to the instructions on the container every two weeks until ⚐

Dendrobium nobile

❧

What You Need
30-10-10 orchid fertilizer,
diluted half-strength

❧

When to Buy
In bloom

❧

Light
Morning or afternoon sun
during winter months
Summer outside in the brightest part of a
lathhouse or bright, dappled shade

❧

Water and Humidity
Begin watering in spring as temperatures
rise above 50°F
Twice-weekly watering through growing
season, more often in heat spells
Monthly watering when temperature drops
to 50°F, about October

❧

Fertilizing Schedule
Every 2 weeks from spring until October

❧

Hardiness
To 40°F

❧

When Blooms Appear
March to May

❧

October. Increase watering during spring, until during midsummer heat you are watering almost daily to make sure the plant does not dry out. In October stop fertilizing and begin to reduce watering to only once a month until the buds swell in the spring. Once you see the buds, begin to water and fertilize the nobile again. ¶ Use medium-coarse orchid bark and lava rocks as a potting mix, and repot after three years if the mix has broken down to a fine texture. Repot only after bloom finishes and new growth starts. ¶ As plants come into bloom, make sure to stake the stems. If you bring them inside while they flower, place them out of direct sunlight in a cool room but continue watering to extend the blossom period.

MASDEVALLIA

These orchids look more like underwater creatures, sea anemones, or strangely bearded fish with long, swirling fins. Many varieties flash neon-bright colors like a shoal of tropical fish caught for an instant, motionless. Here again, the ingenuity of nature's design awes and puzzles: How did the standard orchid flower ingredients end up configured as this extraordinarily shaped flower that's totally different from a mainstream orchid? ¶ Many of the masdevallias come from high Andean mountain slopes smothered in misty, moisty clouds, and these types accept only cool, high-altitude temperatures, making them unsuitable for home climates. Yet masdevallias that live as epiphytes on trees closer to sea level, the warm-growing types, adjust easily to home culture, and the plants stay conveniently small. ¶ Masdevallias need to be kept moist, which, because they grow in quite small pots, is not as easy as it sounds. You will have to water twice a week during winter, and more often in summer. Plastic or glazed ceramic pots retain moisture most effectively and are good choices for your masdevallias. They don't need much feeding; if overfertilized, the tips of their leaves turn brown. Make sure you take home a warm-growing masdevallia. Repot only in spring about every two years. ¶ **HOW TO DO IT** ¶ During the winter months, keep your masdevallia on a north-facing windowsill, where your hand does not cast a shadow. The foliage should be light green, dark green indicating too little light. Place the pot on gravel in a saucer filled with water. In the summer the plant benefits from placement outside in a shady spot, but be sure to maintain a high humidity by keeping the saucer filled with water. Water the plant twice a week, more often during a summer heat spell. Make sure your plant does not dry out between waterings. Feed it once a month with a 30-10-10 fertilizer diluted half-strength according to the directions on the container. Use fine-grade orchid bark as a potting mix, and repot after two years if the mix has broken down to a fine texture.

Masdevallia Hybrid
warm-growing variety

What You Need
*30-10-10 orchid fertilizer
diluted half-strength*

When to Buy
In bloom

Light
*Light shade; your hand should not
cast a shadow
Summer outside in a shady spot*

Water and Humidity
*Water twice weekly, more often in
hot weather
Set container on gravel in a saucer
filled with water*

Fertilizing Schedule
Monthly

Hardiness
Tender

When Blooms Appear
Almost year-round, depending on variety

Maxillaria tenuifolia, Coconut Orchid

The coconut orchid pleases the scamp more than the ascetic, for here is a plant to make anyone in its vicinity suddenly long for fresh coconut cream pie. The reddish blossoms, shaped somewhat like a three-sided hat, exude a rich, tropical fragrance, unmistakably coconut. The blossoms hide low amidst the thin, grassy blades of the plant leaves, but their scent immediately announces their presence. Grown less for its blossoms than its alluring scent, this fragrant plant transforms any locale into a tropical island. ¶ Grow coconut orchid as you would cattleyas, but use a fine-grade potting mix in the container. Sometimes these orchids are sold growing on cork rafts, in which case they need daily watering to keep the roots from drying out. If you prefer, you can repot them after bloom into a container. ¶ **HOW TO DO IT** ¶ During the winter months, provide as much bright sunny light as you can for your coconut orchid by placing it on a south-, east-, or west-facing windowsill, where it will receive bright sun. The foliage should be light green, dark green indicating too little light. Place the pot on gravel in a saucer filled with water. In the summer the plant can be placed outside in a lathhouse or a bright, sun-dappled spot, but be sure to maintain a high humidity by misting during heat spells and keeping the saucer filled with water. Water the plant once a week, twice a week if necessary in a summer heat spell. Feed it every two weeks with a 30-10-10 fertilizer diluted half-strength during the growing season, from March to October, then once a month from November through February. Use medium-grade orchid bark as a potting mix, and repot after two years if the mix has broken down to a fine texture.

Coconut Orchid
Maxillaria tenuifolia

What You Need
30-10-10 orchid fertilizer,
diluted half-strength

When to Buy
In bloom

Light
Morning or afternoon sun
during winter months
Summer outside in a lathhouse
or bright, dappled shade

Water and Humidity
Water weekly, more often in hot weather
Set container over gravel in a saucer
filled with water
Mist daily in the early morning

Fertilizing Schedule
Every 2 weeks

Hardiness
Tender

When Blooms Appear
April to June

MILTONIOPSIS, PANSY ORCHID

As charming as the pansies we fell in love with as children, their flowers seemly as sweet faces, these orchids beguile. However, somewhat like television ads, things are not quite what they seem. Pansy orchids are not as easy to grow as the cheerful flowers cultivated outside our kitchen door in childhood. Not to say you should avoid them, for indeed most orchidophiles cannot. These orchids engage devotees from across the room, inveigle themselves rides home, and seduce themselves into growers' affections. But they need quite specific care to bloom again and, comparisons to fickle lovers who leave after a one-night stand aside, careful attention to their growing needs is critical for success. ¶ Pansy orchids are fussy about temperature, preferring to go from a daytime temperature of around 70 to 75°F down to sweater weather of 55 to 60°F at night. In the summer, they need increased humidity so keep them on saucers with gravel and mist the foliage in the mornings. Give them the shady light conditions of paphiopedilums. Regular watering and regular fertilizing keep them growing and blossoming. Leaves that develop looking as pleated as a tuxedo shirt indicate you are underwatering the plant. ¶ Don't repot your pansy orchid until it crowds the container. Follow the potting procedures for cymbidiums, on page 71. ¶ **HOW TO DO IT** ¶ During the winter months, keep your pansy orchid on a north-facing windowsill, where your hand does not cast a shadow. Place it on gravel in a saucer filled with water. In the summer the plant benefits from placement outside in a shady spot, but be sure to maintain a high humidity by misting and keeping the saucer filled with water. Water the plant once a week, twice a week ✒

Pansy Orchid
Miltoniopsis hybrid

What You Need
30-10-10 orchid fertilizer,
diluted half-strength

When to Buy
In bloom

Light
Light shade; your hand should not
cast a shadow

Water and Humidity
Water weekly, more often in hot weather
Set container on gravel in a saucer filled
with water
Mist daily in the summer

Fertilizing Schedule
Every 2 weeks

Hardiness
To 40°F

When Blooms Appear
November to April

during a summer heat spell. Feed it every two weeks with a 30-10-10 fertilizer diluted half-strength according to the directions on the container. Use a cymbidium mix or one-half coarse-grade orchid bark and one-half container potting mix, and repot after two years if the medium has broken down to a fine texture. ¶ And while they flower, place them out of direct sunlight in a cool room but continue watering to extend bloom.

BLUE-FLOWERED VANDA

Vandas look a bit like fans, their stems upright and the leaves branching out, as if you could grasp the stem and cool yourself off. Some varieties are fussy about temperature, but the blue vanda hybrids, which have been crossed with Vanda coerulea, don't mind the temperature dropping down to 60°F at night. The remarkable sky-blue flowers with checkered lines are simply stunning. Some types grow exceedingly tall, up to 7 feet, so choose one to suit your space. Most grow only 2 feet tall. ¶ What these tropical orchids like is direct light, as much as you can give them. Professionals often use growing lamps to make sure these orchids receive sufficient light to rebloom. Vandas are tropical epiphytes, and in areas with warm days and nights, growers simply prop them up in baskets and let their roots fall out free to the breezes. This type of treatment works as long as you water them daily; but to make your life simpler, you can grow them in coarse orchid bark and water them twice a week. Repot vandas as seldom as possible, every three years at most. Many vanda growers like teak slatted baskets to minimize the need for repotting, for the plants balk at having their roots disturbed and will respond by not flowering for several years. When the plants need a bigger container, they simply slip the basket into a larger one.

¶ **HOW TO DO IT** ¶ During the winter months, keep your vanda on a south-, east-, or west-facing windowsill where it will receive bright sun. The foliage should be light green, dark green indicating too little light. Place the pot on gravel in a saucer filled with water. In the summer the plant benefits from placement outside in a lathhouse or where it receives morning and afternoon sun, but be sure to maintain high humidity by keeping the saucer filled with water. Water the plant twice a week, more often during ✒

Blue-Flowered Vanda Hybrid

🦎

What You Need

30-10-10 orchid fertilizer
diluted half-strength

🦎

When to Buy

In bloom

🦎

Light

Morning or afternoon sun during winter
Summer outside in a lathhouse or bright,
dappled shade

🦎

Water and Humidity

Water twice weekly, more often
in hot weather
Set container on gravel in a saucer
filled with water

🦎

Fertilizing Schedule

Every 2 weeks

🦎

Hardiness

Tender

🦎

When Blooms Appear

March to April

🦎

a summer heat spell. Feed it every two weeks with a 30-10-10 fertilizer diluted half-strength according to the directions on the container. Use coarse-grade orchid bark as a potting mix and repot after three years only if the medium has broken down to a fine texture. ¶ As plants come into bloom, make sure to stake the blossoms. And while they flower, place them out of direct sunlight in a cool room but continue watering to extend the blossom period.

Vanilla planifolia, vanilla orchid

The Spaniards were the first Europeans to discover vanilla. During their conquest of the Americas, they came across an exotic fruit from a vining orchid used in Aztec cooking and especially with chocolate. The Aztecs, true epicures, called the fruit tlilxochitl, a tongue twister that the Spanish incorrectly translated to vainilla or baynilla, meaning "little pod." There are a number of vanilla orchid species that grow throughout Mexico, Central America, and South America. The tall, twining plants bear fruit vibrantly fragrant. Workers scrambling up trees to gather fruit from the vine allegedly often swoon from the intoxicating perfume—hazardous for the worker 60 feet or more up a tree at the time. ¶ Consider adding a vanilla to your orchid collection for its flower fragrance, bloom, and seedpod. Yet don't forget its vining characteristics. This is no mild-mannered windowsill orchid, but a sprawling tangle of growth, unfurling green arms all over the walls. You will need a generously sized, warm, and brightly lit indoor space to house a vanilla orchid. Make sure to support the branches with ties loosely looped around the plant and fastened to a structure. Look for Vanilla planifolia, a small, contained variety. Other vanilla types may grow up to 100 feet long. ¶ Flowers are borne only on mature plants, usually after they have grown at least 15 feet, so expect to wait two years or more before blooms appear. With careful hand-pollination using a toothpick, you may be able to harvest your own vanilla beans, although human pollinators have less success than the natural ones. Work in the morning, lifting the flap over the stigma and gently prick up a pollen clump from one of the yellowy green flowers and place it on the pistil of a different flower. When the capsules form and turn yellow on the bottom, detach them from the plant and allow them to dry in a warm place out of direct sunlight. ¶ **HOW TO DO IT** ¶ Carefully choose a space to fit the requirements of the plant: a brightly lit room with a wall to support the vine and a high level of humidity. Provide strong support for growing stems, ✒

Vanilla Orchid
Vanilla planifolia
❧

What You Need
30-10-10 orchid fertilizer, diluted half-strength
Plant ties
Plant support
❧

When to Buy
Anytime
❧

Light
Bright light, but no direct sunlight on the leaves during summer
❧

Water and Humidity
Water twice weekly, more often in hot weather
Set container on gravel in a saucer filled with water
❧

Fertilizing Schedule
Every 2 weeks
❧

Hardiness
Tender
❧

When Blooms Appear
July to September
❧

attaching them as they grow upward. The foliage should be light green, dark green indicating too little light. Place the pot on gravel in a saucer filled with water. Water the plant once a week, twice a week during a summer heat spell. Feed it every two weeks with a 30-10-10 fertilizer diluted half-strength according to the directions on the container. Use a cymbidium mix or one-half coarse-grade orchid bark and one-half container potting mix and repot after three years only if the medium has broken down to a fine texture. ¶ As the flowers appear, use a toothpick to lift the flap over the stigma and gently prick up a pollen clump from one flower and place it on the pistil of a different flower to produce the vanilla pods.

Afterword

The goal of this book has been to demystify orchid growing so that beginners have a starting place to explore the mysteries and magic of orchids. Poring through volumes of technically advanced information, attempting to translate footcandles into sensible home light requirements, and choosing a limited number of "first" orchids has been a maddeningly elusive project driven only by the desire to present a reference to simplify home orchid growing. ¶ My final advice to the new orchid grower is simply to start growing orchids, and as in any new pursuit, keep experimenting, read everything you can, and never stop asking questions. Don't stick with just one plant, but expand your collection to at least a dozen or more with similar growing requirements. If a plant shrivels and dies, don't assume you have a black thumb; take it back to the place you bought it and ask the owner for a diagnosis. ¶ Orchid growing can be easy if you start with "user-friendly" plants, follow a consistent watering and fertilizing program, and provide the appropriate light. This book gives you a foundation; it isn't an all-inclusive, professional-level manual. Once you have established a bond with orchids, you'll uncover many other professionals, books, and magazines to fill out your knowledge.

MAIL-ORDER SOURCES

There are literally hundreds of reputable mail-order sources for orchids from large companies with a diversity of stock to smaller companies specializing in specie orchids. Listed here is a sampling of larger companies shipping a wide variety of orchids. There are smaller companies specializing in more unusual types of orchids so when you develop a passion for a particular orchid type, search these out to widen your collection.

Kensington Orchids
3301 Plyers Mill Rd.
Kensington, MD 20895
301 933-0036
www.kensingtonorchids.com
Free catalogue

Orchid World International
10885 SW 95th Street
Miami, FL 33176
305 271-0268
www.orchidworld.net
Catalogue for fee, refunded with purchase

Santa Barbara Orchid Estates
1250 Orchid Drive
Santa Barbara, CA 93117
805 967-1284
Free catalogue

The Rod McLellan Company
914 South Claremont
San Mateo, CA 94402
650 373-3900
www.rodmclellan.com
Catalogue for fee

Stewart Orchids
PO Box 460
Natchez, MS 39121
800 621-2450
www.stewartorchids.com
Free catalogue

One of the best sources of information about orchids is
The American Orchid Society
16700 AOS Lane
Delray Beach, FL 33446
561 404-2000
www.orchidweb.org
The AOS publishes an informative monthly bulletin, provides an education service, and is in touch with both the national and international orchid scene. Anyone interested in orchids will find membership in this organization very useful.

BIBLIOGRAPHY

American Orchid Society.
Growing Orchids.
West Palm Beach: American
Orchid Society, 1993.

Butterfield, Ian, and Phillip Cribb.
The Genus Pleione.
Bromley, Kent, England: The Royal
Botanic Gardens, Kew, in association
with Christopher Helm and Timber
Press, 1988.

James, I. D.
The Orchid Growers Handbook.
London, England: Blandford, 1990.

Jaworski, Henry.
Orchids Simplified. An Indoor Gardening Guide
Shelburne, VT: Chapters Publishing,
1992.

Marshall, Nina T.
The Gardener's Guide to Plant Conservation.
Washington, D.C.: World Wildlife Fund,
1993.

Northern, Rebecca Tyson.
Orchids as House Plants.
New York: Dover Publications, 1976.

Stewart, Joyce.
Kew Gardening Orchids.
London, England: The Royal Botanic
Gardens, Kew, in association with
Collingridge Books, 1988.

Index

ACKNOWLEDGMENTS

Starting a new book is like embarking on a voyage of discovery, like the early orchid adventurers. Setting out for the unknown with only the map of enthusiasm, we have been guided by seasoned experts who illuminated the unknown and charted us back to safe harbor. ¶ Many expert orchid growers helped us translate orchid lore from the technical to the understandable, dazzled us with their specimens of incredible beauty, and read the manuscript for corrections. The staff and volunteers of the University of California at Berkeley Botanical Gardens were terrifically generous with their time and expertise. Judith Finn and Jerry Parsons on the staff and long-time volunteers Dick Emory, Tom Colby, and Jim H. Jones answered questions and provided the wisdom of their years raising orchids as a hobby and professionally. Thanks to Tomas Vilanova of San Salvador, grower and acknowledged authority for the garden tour. ¶ Michael Serpa of Bay Island Orchids, Alameda, California, also gave us a great deal of his time to discuss orchids and growing techniques and allowed us to photograph in his greenhouses. Rod McLellan Acres of Orchids gave us permission to photograph many magnificent orchid specimens. We are indebted to the talented Ted and Paul of Tesoro, St. Helena, California, whose shop we used as a backdrop, as well as to Linda Good, Tyler and Peggy Ahlgren, Colin Smith of Zia, Katie Sinnes, Martha, Susan, and Debbie. ¶ Keeping us shipshape were our editors Hazel White, Leslie Jonath, Bill LeBlond, and our publicist, David Carriere. Sarah Bolles at Chronicle Books and Aufuldish and Warinner set the sails with a finely crafted book design. Thanks to our agents Mickey Choate and Susan Lescher of The Lescher Agency. We thank, of course, those who kept the home fires burning, Bruce LeFavour, and Arann and Daniel Harris.